MW00887373

Preston Lee's

2-in-1 BOOK SERIES!

Beginner ENGLISH + Conversation ENGLISH

Lesson 1 - 40

For Russian Speakers

Preston Lee Books

prestonleebooks@gmail.com

No unauthorized photocopying

All rights reserved. No part of this publication may be reproduced, stored in a retrieval system, or transmitted, in any form or by any means, without the prior permission in writing of Preston Lee Books.

This book is sold subject to the condition that it shall not, by the way of trade or otherwise, be lent, resold, hired out, or otherwise circulated without the publisher's prior consent in any form of binding or cover than that in which it is published and without a similar condition including this condition being imposed on the subsequent purchaser.

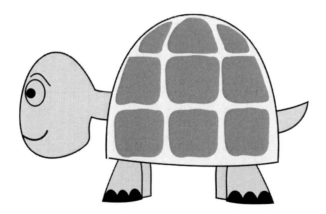

Copyright © 2019 Matthew Preston, Kevin Lee
All rights reserved.

ISBN: 9781679234934
Imprint: Independently published

Preston Lee's

Beginner
ENGLISH

Page 4

Preston Lee's

Conversation
ENGLISH

Lesson 1 - 40

Page 209

Preston Lee's

Beginner
ENGLISH

For Russian Speakers

CONTENTS

Lesson 1: My family моя семья   Page 8

Lesson 2: My pencil case мой пенал   Page 12

Lesson 3: In the classroom в классе   Page 16

Lesson 4: The weather погода   Page 20

Test 1   Lesson 1 - 4   Page 24

Lesson 5: Places места   Page 26

Lesson 6: Sports спорт   Page 30

Lesson 7: At the zoo в зоопарке   Page 34

Lesson 8: Colors цвета   Page 38

Test 2   Lesson 5 - 8   Page 42

Lesson 9: Activities занятия   Page 44

Lesson 10: Food & Drinks еда и напитки   Page 48

Lesson 11: At a fruit market на фруктовом рынке   Page 52

Lesson 12: Shapes фигуры   Page 56

Test 3   Lesson 9 - 12   Page 60

Lesson 13: At the supermarket в супермаркете   Page 62
Lesson 14: Ice cream shop в магазине мороженого   Page 66
Lesson 15: In the refrigerator в холодильнике   Page 70
Lesson 16: Jobs работа   Page 74

Test 4   Lesson 13 - 16   Page 78

Lesson 17: Names имена   Page 80
Lesson 18: More places еще места   Page 84
Lesson 19: Meats мясо   Page 88
Lesson 20: Vegetables овощи   Page 92

Test 5   Lesson 17 - 20   Page 96

Lesson 21: At school в школе   Page 98
Lesson 22: School subjects школьные предметы   Page 102
Lesson 23: Chores работа по дому   Page 106
Lesson 24: At the toy store в магазине игрушек   Page 110

Test 6   Lesson 21 - 24   Page 114

Lesson 25: In the kitchen в кухне   Page 116
Lesson 26: Toolbox в ящике для инструментов   Page 120
Lesson 27: Transportation транспорт   Page 124
Lesson 28: Clothes одежда   Page 128

Test 7   Lesson 25 - 28   Page 132

Lesson 29: More clothes ещё одежда — Page 134

Lesson 30: In the living room в гостиной — Page 138

Lesson 31: In the bathroom в ванной комнате — Page 142

Lesson 32: In the bedroom в спальне — Page 146

Test 8 | Lesson 29 - 32 — Page 150

Lesson 33: Around the house возле дома — Page 152

Lesson 34: Hobbies хобби — Page 156

Lesson 35: Countries страны — Page 160

Lesson 36: Landscapes ландшафты — Page 164

Test 9 | Lesson 33 - 36 — Page 168

Lesson 37: Everyday life повседневная жизнь — Page 170

Lesson 38: Languages языки — Page 174

Lesson 39: Pets домашние любимцы — Page 178

Lesson 40: Fast food фаст-фуд — Page 182

Test 10 | Lesson 37 - 40 — Page 186

Lesson 41: At the cinema в кинотеатре — Page 188

Lesson 42: Music музыка — Page 192

Lesson 43: Feelings чувства — Page 196

Lesson 44: The calendar календарь — Page 200

Test 11 | Lesson 41 - 44 — Page 204

Answers | Test 1 - 11 — Page 206

Lesson 1: My family

моя семья

Who is she?

She is my baby sister.

Section A	Words

1. **mother**
   мать
2. **grandmother**
   бабушка
3. **sister**
   сестра
4. **baby sister**
   сестренка
5. **aunt**
   тётя

6. **father**
   отец
7. **grandfather**
   дедушка
8. **brother**
   брат
9. **baby brother**
   братишка
10. **uncle**
    дядя

Section B	Make a sentence

Who is <u>she</u>?

She is my <u>mother</u>.

Who is <u>he</u>?

He is my <u>father</u>.

Note: isn't = is not

Is <u>she</u> your <u>mother</u>?

Yes, she is. / No, she isn't.

Is <u>he</u> your <u>father</u>?

Yes, he is. / No, he isn't.

see – seeing – saw – seen видеть

He **sees** my father on Fridays.

I will be **seeing** him this afternoon.

My brother **saw** you yesterday.

I haven't **seen** that movie yet.

Like one of the family

Meaning: To be like a person in one's family.

"Our dog is treated *like one of the family*."

Trace and write the words

1. Who is she?

She is my mother.

2. Who _____ he?

He is my father.

3. Who _____ _____?

She _____ my grandmother.

4. Who _____ _____?

He _____ _____ grandfather.

5. Is she your sister?

Yes, she is.

6. Is _____ your brother?

No, he isn't.

7. Is she your mother?

Yes, _____ _____.

8. Is _____ _____ father?

_____, _____ _____.

My family!

Find the words!

```
c i o b j t d c z b g g r o v k
o i j m w d o g f a j r k s s q
q d e g q l z t c b z a q c u o
u w n r c e o z s y i n t t t v
n f f a t h e r o b a d y s y r
c d l n b h j m u r x f d v t q
l z a d m g g y e o x a c m n v
e h p m o t h e r t z t j y t f
f u e o v q q f d h e h b x s n
n z v t u x l w j e z e k o u v
t a a h s i s t e r o r y a l r
t o u e y v s h b r o t h e r j
j n n r u d o s x j v t y k y o
j b t y t d b a b y s i s t e r
```

mother   brother
father   baby sister
grandmother   baby brother
grandfather   aunt
sister   uncle

Lesson 2: My pencil case

мой пенал

What is this?

It is an eraser.

1. **a pencil**
   карандаш
2. **an eraser**
   ластик
3. **glue**
   клей
4. **a pencil sharpener**
   точилка
5. **whiteout**
   корректор

6. **a pen**
   ручка
7. **a ruler**
   линейка
8. **tape**
   липкая лента
9. **a marker**
   маркер
10. **a crayon**
    мелок

Section B | Make a sentence

What is this?

It is <u>a pencil</u>.

What are these?

They are <u>pen</u>s.

Is this <u>an eraser</u>?

Yes, it is. / No, it isn't.

Are these <u>ruler</u>s?

Yes, they are. / No, they aren't.

buy – buying – bought – bought покупать

I will **buy** some pencils for you.

My sister was **buying** a new ruler.

My father **bought** an eraser.

My mother hasn't **bought** some glue yet.

Cross your fingers

Meaning: To wish for luck.

"*Cross your fingers* and hope this marker has ink."

Trace and write the words

1. What is this?

It is a pencil.

2. What _____ these?

They are pens.

3. What _____ _____?

It _____ a ruler.

4. What _____ _____?

They _____ markers.

5. Is this an eraser?

Yes, it is.

6. Is _____ a pencil sharpener?

No, it isn't.

7. Is _____ a crayon?

No, _____ isn't.

8. _____ _____ rulers?

Yes, _____ _____.

My pencil case!

Unscramble the words!

1. encpil   <u>pencil</u>

2. enp

3. relru

4. eugl

5. reshrapne cpneli

6. arerse

7. emrakr

8. hwteituo

9. yocarn

10. ptae

Lesson 3: In the Classroom

в классе

What are these?
These are old books.

Section A   Words

1. **chair**
   стул
2. **blackboard**
   доска для мела
3. **poster**
   плакат
4. **globe**
   глобус
5. **clock**
   часы

6. **desk**
   парта
7. **whiteboard**
   доска для маркера
8. **bookshelf**
   книжная полка
9. **computer**
   компьютер
10. **book**
    книга

Section B   Make a sentence

What is this?

This is a <u>big</u> <u>chair</u>.

What are these?

These are <u>small</u> <u>desk</u>s.

Learn: big, small, new, old

Is the <u>blackboard</u> <u>big</u>?

Yes, it is. / No, it is <u>small</u>.

Are the <u>desk</u>s <u>new</u>?

Yes, they are. / No, they are <u>old</u>.

look – looking – looked – looked смотреть, выглядеть

Please **look** at the blackboard.

They are **looking** at the whiteboard.

My father **looked** at your bicycle yesterday.

We have already **looked** at many houses.

Class clown

Meaning: A student who often makes everyone laugh in the classroom.

"Peter is the *class clown*. Even the teacher laughs sometimes."

Trace and write the words

1. What is this?

This is a big chair.

2. What _____ these?

These are small desks.

3. What _____ _____?

This is a _____ _____.

4. What _____ _____?

These are _____ _____.

5. Is the blackboard big?

Yes, it is.

6. Are _____ desks new?

No, they _____ old.

7. Is the _____ small?

No, it is big.

8. Are the _____ _____?

Yes, _____ _____.

In the classroom!

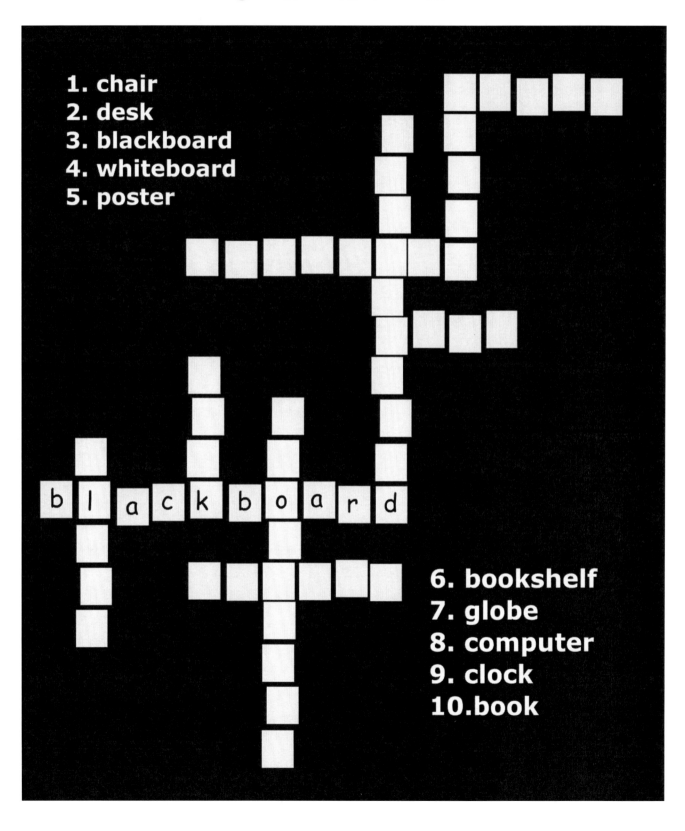

1. chair
2. desk
3. blackboard
4. whiteboard
5. poster

6. bookshelf
7. globe
8. computer
9. clock
10. book

Lesson 4: The weather

погода

How is the weather on Friday?

It is sunny.

Words

1. **snowy**
   снег
2. **sunny**
   солнечно
3. **rainy**
   дождливо
4. **windy**
   ветрено
5. **cloudy**
   облачно

6. **hot**
   жарко
7. **cold**
   холодно
8. **warm**
   тепло
9. **cool**
   прохладно
10. **freezing**
    морозно

Section B Make a sentence

How is the weather on <u>Monday</u>?

It is <u>snowy</u>.

It is not <u>hot</u>.

Learn: Sunday, Monday, Tuesday, Wednesday, Thursday, Friday, Saturday

Is the weather <u>cold</u> on <u>Wednesday</u>?

Yes, it is. / No, it isn't. It is <u>hot</u>.

Is the weather <u>sunny</u>?

Yes, it is. / No, it isn't. It is <u>rainy</u>.

feel – feeling – felt – felt чувствовать

My sister always **feels** tired after school.

I'm not **feeling** well.

I **felt** something on the back of my neck.

I haven't **felt** this happy for a long time!

It's raining cats and dogs

Meaning: It's raining heavily.

"You can't play outside right now. *It's raining cats and dogs.*"

Trace and write the words

1. How is the weather on Monday?

It is snowy.

2. How is the weather _____ Thursday?

It is cloudy. It _____ not rainy.

3. How is the _____ _____ Friday?

It is _____.

4. How is _____ _____ _____ Tuesday?

It is cold. It is _____ _____.

5. Is the _____ hot?

Yes, it _____.

6. Is _____ _____ windy on Wednesday?

No, it isn't. It is _____.

7. Is the _____ _____ on Saturday?

Yes, _____ _____.

8. Is the weather _____?

No, it _____. It is _____.

The weather!

snowy	sunny	rainy	windy	cloudy
hot	cold	warm	cool	freezing

Write the words

Sunday	Monday	Tuesday	Wednesday	Thursday	Friday	Saturday
Ra_n_	W_n_y	Cl_u_y	S_n_y	C_ _d	H_ _	W_r_

Circle the correct answer

1. Is the weather cold on Thursday?

Yes, it is.　　　　No, it's not. It's hot.

2. Is the weather windy on Monday?

Yes, it is.　　　　No, it's not. It's hot.

3. Is the weather rainy on Wednesday?

Yes, it is.　　　　No, it's not. It's sunny.

4. Is the weather cold on Friday?

Yes, it is.　　　　No, it's not. It's hot.

Write the answer next to the letter "A"

A: ___ **1.** Who ___ she? She is ___ mother.

a. is, my   b. are, her   c. am, his   d. is, me

A: ___ **2.** ___ he your father? Yes, ___ is.

a. Is, she   b. Are, he   c. Is, he   d. Are, she

A: ___ **3.** We ___ a movie now.

a. are seeing   b. seen   c. is seeing   d. saw

A: ___ **4.** "The housekeeper is one ___ the family."

a. off   b. is   c. from   d. of

A: ___ **5.** What are ___? ___ are markers.

a. this, They   b. these, It   c. it, They   d. these, They

A: ___ **6.** Are ___ rulers? No, ___ aren't.

a. it, these   b. them, it   c. these, they d. this, it

A: ___ **7.** I ___ a pencil yesterday.

a. buy   b. buying   c. bought   d. buys

A: ___ **8.** Tom: "I hope I pass my test." Mary: "___ your fingers."

a. Hold   b. Cross   c. Pull   d. Look at

A: ___ **9.** What ___ these? These are ___ posters.

a. are, those   b. is, small   c. is, old   d. are, big

A: ___ **10.** Is the ___ small? No, it is ___.

a. it, old   b. globe, big   c. chair, desk   d. this, new

A: ___ **11.** He is ___ at the whiteboard.

a. looks   b. looking   c. looked   d. look

A: ___ **12.** "Johnny is the class ___. He's so funny."

a. clown   b. clowned   c. clowning   d. clowns

A: ___ **13.** How is the ___ on Tuesday? It is ___. It is not hot.

a. weather, cold   b. rainy, sunny   c. cool, old   d. hot, rain

A: ___ **14.** Is the weather ___ on Friday? Yes, ___ is.

a. cold, it   b. cold, snowy c. hot, sunny   d. it, cold

A: ___ **15.** She ___ feel cold.

a. very   b. isn't   c. doesn't   d. do

A: ___ **16.** "Look at the heavy rain. It's raining ___ and ___."

a. lots, water   b. dogs, cats   c. cat, dog   d. cats, dogs

Answers on page 206

Lesson 5: Places

места

Where is he going?
He is going to the gym.

1. **park**
   парк
2. **beach**
   пляж
3. **night market**
   ночной рынок
4. **store**
   магазин
5. **supermarket**
   супермаркет

6. **restaurant**
   ресторан
7. **swimming pool**
   бассейн
8. **department store**
   универмаг
9. **cinema**
   кинотеатр
10. **gym**
    спортзал

Section B | Make a sentence

Where is <u>she</u> going?

She is going to the <u>park</u>.

Where is <u>he</u> going?

He is going to the <u>beach</u>.

Is <u>he</u> going to the <u>store</u>?

Yes, he is. / No, he isn't.

Is <u>she</u> going to the <u>supermarket</u>?

Yes, she is. / No, she isn't.

walk – walking – walked – walked ходить

I **walk** at the park on Sundays.

She will be **walking** to the store tomorrow morning.

My grandmother **walked** to the supermarket last week.

I've never **walked** to the night market before.

Have a change of heart

Meaning: To change your mind about something.

"I've *had a change of heart* about this place. Let's go to another restaurant."

Trace and fill in the words

1. Where is she going?

She is going to the park.

2. Where is he going?

He is going to the beach.

3. Where is _____ _____?

She is going to the _____.

4. Where is _____ _____?

He is _____ to the _____.

5. Is he going to the store?

Yes, he is.

6. Is she going to the gym?

No, she isn't.

7. Is he going to the _____?

Yes, _____ is.

8. Is she going to the _____?

No, _____ _____.

Places!

1. Where is he going?

He is going to the department store.

2. Where is she going?

_____

3. Where is he going?

_____

4. Where is she going?

_____

5. Where is he going?

_____

Lesson 6: Sports

спорт

What are you playing?
I am playing golf.

1. **basketball**
   баскетбол
2. **soccer**
   футбол
3. **badminton**
   бадминтон
4. **golf**
   гольф
5. **hockey**
   хоккей

6. **cricket**
   крикет
7. **tennis**
   теннис
8. **baseball**
   бейсбол
9. **volleyball**
   воллейбол
10. **football**
    футбол

Section B — Make a sentence

What are <u>you</u> playing?

I am playing <u>basketball</u>.

What are <u>they</u> playing?

They are playing <u>soccer</u>.

Note: aren't = are not / I'm = I am

Are <u>you</u> playing <u>basketball</u>?

Yes, I am. / No, I'm not.

Are <u>they</u> playing <u>soccer</u>?

Yes, they are. / No, they aren't.

play – playing – played – played играть

I **play** basketball at the park on the weekends.

She will be **playing** tennis in the school competition.

My brother and I **played** badminton last night.

My grandfather has **played** golf for a long time.

A good sport

Meaning: Someone who can accept losing or be made fun of.

"We made fun of Johnny, but he was *a good sport* and laughed with us."

Trace and fill in the words

1. What _____ you playing?

_____ am _____ basketball.

2. _____ is _____ playing?

She _____ playing tennis.

3. What are they _____?

They are playing _____.

4. What _____ they _____?

_____ are playing _____.

5. _____ you playing volleyball?

Yes, _____ am.

6. _____ she _____ football?

No, _____ isn't.

7. Are they playing _____?

Yes, _____ are.

8. Are we playing _____?

No, _____ _____.

Section G Let's have fun

Sports!

Connect the sentences

What are you playing? •   •We are playing soccer.

What are they playing? •   • I am playing tennis.

What are you playing? •   • He is playing basketball.

What is he playing? •   • They are playing baseball.

Are you playing golf? •   • No, she isn't.

Is she playing hockey? •   • Yes, they are.

Is he playing football? •   • Yes, I am.

Are they playing volleyball? •   • No, he isn't.

Lesson 7: At the zoo

в зоопарке

How many lions are there?

There are two lions.

Section A — Words

1. **monkey**
   обезьяна
2. **lion**
   лев
3. **tiger**
   тигр
4. **rhino**
   носорог
5. **bear**
   медведь

6. **penguin**
   пингвин
7. **giraffe**
   жираф
8. **elephant**
   слон
9. **kangaroo**
   кенгуру
10. **crocodile**
    крокодил

Section B — Make a sentence

How many <u>monkeys</u> are there?

There is one monkey.

There are <u>three</u> monkeys.

Learn: one, two, three, four, five, six, seven, eight, nine, ten

Note: there's = there is

Is there one <u>rhino</u>?

Yes, there is. / No, there isn't.

Are there <u>five</u> <u>bears</u>?

Yes, there are. / No, there aren't.

like – liking – liked – liked любить, нравиться

I **like** the kangaroo.

The penguins are **liking** the new fish.

We **liked** the lions best at the zoo yesterday.

The bear hasn't **liked** any of the food we prepared.

Let the cat out of the bag

Meaning: To let someone know a secret.

"He let the cat out of the bag about the surprise party."

Trace and fill in the words

1. How many monkeys are there?

There is one monkey.

2. How many penguins are there?

There _____ five penguins.

3. How many _____ are there?

There _____ one _____.

4. How many _____ are there?

There _____ six _____.

5. Is there one rhino?

Yes, there is.

6. Are there four bears?

No, there aren't.

7. Is there one _____?

Yes, there _____.

8. Are there four _____?

No, _____ _____.

At the zoo!

Read and write

ANIMAL	AMOUNT
Monkey	6
Giraffe	
Lion	
Tiger	
Penguin	
Elephant	
Bear	
Kangaroo	
Crocodile	

1. How many monkeys are there?
   There are six monkeys.

2. How many giraffes are there?
   There are four giraffes.

3. How many lions are there?
   There is one lion.

4. How many penguins are there?
   There are seven penguins.

5. How many elephants are there?
   There are two elephants.

6. How many bears are there?
   There is one bear.

7. How many kangaroos are there?
   There are three kangaroos.

8. How many crocodiles are there?
   There is one crocodile.

9. How many tigers are there?
   There are four tigers.

Lesson 8: Colors

цвета

What is your favorite color?

My favorite color is red.

Section A | Words

1. **red**
   красный
2. **blue**
   голубой
3. **orange**
   оранжевый
4. **pink**
   розовый
5. **black**
   черный

6. **yellow**
   желтый
7. **green**
   зеленый
8. **purple**
   лиловый
9. **brown**
   коричневый
10. **white**
    белый

Section B | Make a sentence

What color is this?

It is <u>red</u>.

What is your favorite color?

My favorite color is <u>yellow</u>.

Note: it's = it is

Is this <u>pencil</u> <u>purple</u>?

Yes, it is. / No, it's <u>blue</u>.

Is your favorite color <u>green</u>?

Yes, it is. / No, it isn't.

draw – drawing – drew – drawn рисовать

My uncle can **draw** a green crocodile.

She is **drawing** a black bear.

The teacher **drew** a pink elephant on the blackboard.

I had first **drawn** a brown monkey, but didn't like it.

Feeling blue

Meaning: Feeling unhappy.

"He's *feeling blue* today because he lost the game."

Trace and fill in the words

1. What color is this?

It is green.

2. What _____ your favorite color?

My favorite color is purple.

3. What color is _____?

It is _____.

4. What is your favorite _____?

My _____ color is _____.

5. Is this pencil blue?

Yes, it is.

6. Is your favorite color pink?

No, it isn't.

7. Is this eraser _____?

No, it's _____.

8. Is your favorite color _____?

Yes, it _____.

Colors!

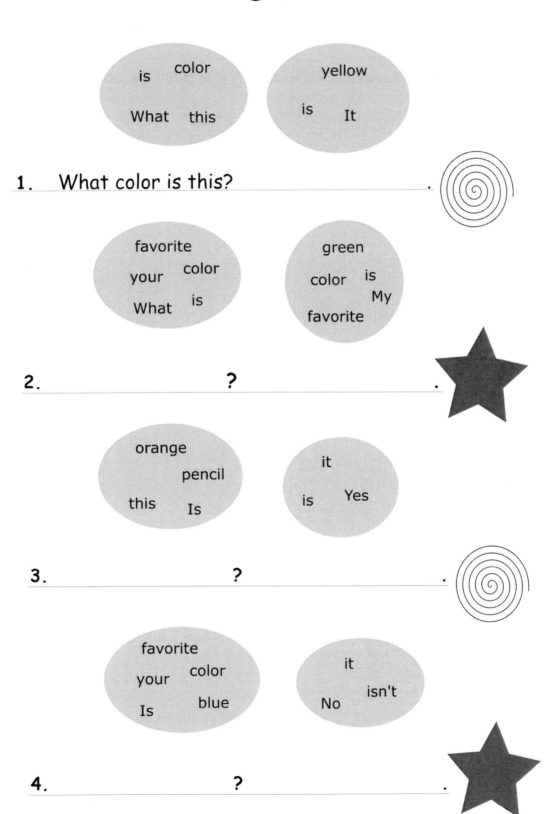

1. What color is this? _____ .

2. _____ ? .

3. _____ ? .

4. _____ ? .

Write the answer next to the letter "A"

A: ___ **1.** Where ___ she going? She is ___ to the beach.

a. does, going   b. is, going   c. are, go   d. is, go

A: ___ **2.** Is ___ going to the store? Yes, she ___ .

a. we, can   b. her, is   c. she, is   d. he, is

A: ___ **3.** Yesterday, they ___ to the cinema.

a. are walk   b. walk   c. walked   d. walking

A: ___ **4.** "I changed my mind about going. I had a change of ___ ."

a. eyes   b. think   c. clothes   d. heart

A: ___ **5.** What are ___ playing? We ___ playing tennis.

a. you, are   b. we, is   c. they, can   d. she, are

A: ___ **6.** ___ you playing soccer? No, ___ not.

a. Is, she's   b. Are, I'm   c. Can, can   d. Are, he's

A: ___ **7.** They want to ___ baseball.

a. played   b. playing   c. plays   d. play

A: ___ **8.** "We laughed at John, but he was a ___ sport."

a. well   b. good   c. easy   d. difficult

A: ___ **9.** How many ___ are there? There ___ two tigers.

a. tiger, are   b. number, is   c. tiger, is   d. tigers, are

A: ___ **10.** Is ___ one kangaroo? No, there ___ .

a. there, isn't   b. number, isn't   c. this, is   d. this, aren't

A: ___ **11.** He ___ the penguins.

a. like   b. liking   c. likes   d. was like

A: ___ **12.** "He told everyone my secret and let the cat ___ the bag."

a. out from   b. into   c. out of   d. out

A: ___ **13.** What is your ___ color? My favorite color ___ purple.

a. best, is   b. best, are   c. favorite, are   d. favorite, is

A: ___ **14.** Is this desk ___? Yes, ___ is.

a. red, they   b. color, pink   c. green, it   d. yellow, he

A: ___ **15.** She can ___ a yellow lion.

a. drawing   b. draw   c. draws   d. drew

A: ___ **16.** "I'm pretty unhappy today. I'm feeling ___ ."

a. red   b. green   c. color   d. blue

Answers on page 206

Lesson 9: Activities

занятия

What do you like to do?

I like to read books.

1. **play piano**
   играть на пианино
2. **read books**
   читать книги
3. **play video games**
   играть в видеоигры
4. **surf the internet**
   бродить по интернету
5. **take photos**
   снимать фотографии

6. **watch TV**
   смотреть ТВ
7. **sing songs**
   петь песни
8. **study English**
   изучать английский
9. **play cards**
   играть в карты
10. **go shopping**
    ходить за покупками

Section B Make a sentence

What do you like to do?

I like to <u>play piano</u>.

What don't you like to do?

I don't like to <u>sing songs</u>.

Note: don't = do not

44

Do you like to <u>play video games</u>?

Yes, I do. / No, I don't.

Don't you like to <u>read books</u>?

Yes, I do. / No, I don't.

read – reading – read – read читать

I can **read** English books.

My sister was **reading** the newspaper this morning.

I **read** a really interesting article last week.

My brother hasn't **read** this book yet.

Shop around

Meaning: To shop at different stores to find the best price.

"You should *shop around* before you buy this piano."

Trace and fill in the words

1. What do you like to do?

I like to read books.

2. What don't you like to do?

I don't like to _____ cards.

3. What do you _____ to do?

I like to _____ _____.

4. What don't you like to _____?

I don't like to _____ _____.

5. Do you like to take photos?

No, I _____.

6. Don't you like to go shopping?

Yes, I do.

7. Do you like to _____ _____?

Yes, I _____.

8. Don't you like to _____ _____?

No, I _____.

Activities!

Unscramble the sentences!

like to / video games / I / play

1. _____.

I / like to / read books / don't

2. _____.

I / study English / like / to

3. _____.

don't / go shopping / I / like to

4. _____.

like / take / I / photos / to

5. _____.

the / don't / I / to / like / internet / surf

6. _____.

Lesson 10: Food & Drinks

еда и напитки

How much tea is there?

There is a lot of tea.

Section A — Words

1. **cake**
   пирожное
2. **cheese**
   сыр
3. **milk**
   молоко
4. **tea**
   чай
5. **soda**
   газировка

6. **pizza**
   пицца
7. **water**
   вода
8. **juice**
   сок
9. **coffee**
   кофе
10. **pie**
   пирог

Section B — Make a sentence

How much <u>cake</u> is there?

There is <u>a little</u> cake.

How much <u>pizza</u> is there?

There is <u>a lot of</u> pizza.

Learn: a little, a lot of

Is there a lot of <u>juice</u>?

Yes, there is. / No, there isn't.

Is there a little <u>water</u>?

Yes, there is. / No, there isn't.

want – wanting – wanted – wanted хотеть

I **want** a lot of tea.

Wanting to improve your English takes practice.

They **wanted** a cheese cake, but the shop didn't have one.

My father has **wanted** to eat pizza all week.

Put food on the table

Meaning: To make money for the household expenses.

"I need this job to *put food on the table*."

Trace and fill in the words

1. How much juice is there?

There is a little juice.

2. How much coffee is there?

There _____ a lot of coffee.

3. How much _____ is there?

There is a _____ _____.

4. How much _____ is there?

There is a _____ of _____.

5. Is there a lot of cheese?

Yes, there is.

6. Is _____ a little tea?

No, there isn't.

7. Is there a _____ of _____?

Yes, there _____.

8. Is _____ a little _____?

No, _____ _____.

Food + Drinks!

Circle the odd word

1. cake   pizza   cheese   (soda)   pie

2. soda   tea   cake   juice   milk

3. pizza   coffee   cheese   pie   cake

4. pie   soda   water   tea   coffee

5. cheese   cake   tea   pie   pizza

6. pizza   milk   coffee   juice   water

7. cake   juice   cheese   pie   pizza

8. water   soda   milk   juice   cheese

Write the word

1.
2.
3.
4.

5.
6.
7.
8.

Lesson 11: At the fruit market

на фруктовом рынке

> **What do you want?**
>
> **I want an apple.**

Section A	Words

1. **orange**
   апельсин
2. **pear**
   груша
3. **watermelon**
   арбуз
4. **strawberry**
   клубника
5. **cherry**
   вишня

6. **lemon**
   лимон
7. **banana**
   банан
8. **grape**
   виноград
9. **pineapple**
   ананас
10. **apple**
    яблоко

Section B	Make a sentence

What do you want?

I want an <u>orange</u>.

What don't you want?

I don't want a <u>lemon</u>.

Note: Say *an* before all words that begin with a, e, i, o, u.

Is there one <u>pear</u>?

Yes, there is. / No, there isn't.

Are there <u>five</u> <u>grapes</u>?

Yes, there are. / No, there aren't.

need – needing – needed – needed нуждаться

I **need** two watermelons for the picnic.

People **needing** vitamin C should eat more oranges.

Yesterday, I **needed** to buy some apples.

I haven't **needed** to use the heater this year.

A bad apple

Meaning: The one bad person in a good group.

"He is *a bad apple* on this basketball team."

Trace and fill in the words

1. What do you want?

I want an apple.

2. What don't you want?

I don't _____ a cherry.

3. What _____ you want?

I want a _____.

4. What _____ you _____?

I don't _____ a _____.

5. Is there one grape?

Yes, there is.

6. Are there seven strawberries?

No, there aren't.

7. Is _____ one _____?

No, _____ isn't.

8. Are _____ three _____?

Yes, _____ _____.

At the fruit market!

Write the missing word

> orange   lemon   pear   strawberry   banana
>
> watermelon   grape   pineapple   cherry   apple

1. orange

- lemon
- pear
- strawberry
- pineapple
- watermelon
- apple
- cherry
- banana
- grape

2. _____

- apple
- orange
- strawberry
- banana
- pear
- lemon
- grape
- pineapple
- cherry

3. _____

- strawberry
- apple
- orange
- watermelon
- pineapple
- pear
- cherry
- banana
- grape

4. _____

- lemon
- pear
- strawberry
- orange
- watermelon
- apple
- cherry
- banana
- pineapple

5. _____

- lemon
- grape
- strawberry
- pineapple
- watermelon
- apple
- cherry
- orange
- banana

6. _____

- pear
- orange
- watermelon
- banana
- strawberry
- apple
- cherry
- lemon
- grape

7. _____

- grape
- pear
- orange
- pineapple
- watermelon
- apple
- banana
- cherry
- lemon

8. _____

- lemon
- pear
- strawberry
- cherry
- watermelon
- banana
- orange
- pineapple
- grape

Lesson 12: Shapes

фигуры

What color is this circle?

This is a green circle.

Section A — Words

1. **square**
   квадрат
2. **circle**
   круг
3. **star**
   звезда
4. **heart**
   сердце
5. **octagon**
   восьмиугольник

6. **triangle**
   треугольник
7. **rectangle**
   прямоугольник
8. **oval**
   овал
9. **diamond**
   ромб
10. **pentagon**
    пятиугольник

Section B — Make a sentence

What color is this <u>square</u>?

This is a <u>red</u> square.

What color is that <u>triangle</u>?

That is a <u>blue</u> triangle.

Is this <u>circle</u> <u>green</u>?

Yes, it is. / No, it isn't. It's <u>blue</u>.

Is that <u>rectangle</u> <u>orange</u>?

Yes, it is. / No, it isn't. It's <u>purple</u>.

find – finding – found – found находить

I can't **find** my keys.

The teacher is **finding** many mistakes in my homework.

I **found** my grandfather's watch.

He still hasn't **found** his workbook.

Be out of shape

Meaning: To be unfit or overweight.

"He can't climb this mountain. He *is* really *out of shape*!"

Trace and fill in the words

1. What color is this rectangle?

This is a yellow rectangle.

2. What color is that oval?

_____ is a green oval.

3. What _____ is _____ diamond?

This is a _____ diamond.

4. _____ color _____ that _____?

_____ _____ a _____ heart.

5. Is this circle purple?

Yes, it is.

6. _____ that octagon blue?

No, _____ _____. It's pink.

7. Is this _____ _____?

Yes, _____ _____.

8. _____ that _____ red?

No, _____ _____. It's _____.

Shapes!

1. What color is this rectangle?

 This is a blue rectangle.   .

blue

2. What color is this star?

_____ .

red

3. What color is this circle?

_____ .

gray

4. What color is this oval?

_____ .

purple

5. What color is this diamond?

_____ .

black

6. What color is this square?

_____ .

blue

7. What color is this pentagon?

_____ .

green

8. What color is this triangle?

_____ .

pink

Write the answer next to the letter "A"

A: ___ **1.** What ___ you like to do? I like to ___ piano.

a. does, do   b. is, play   c. are, go   d. do, play

A: ___ **2.** Don't ___ like to play cards? Yes, I ___.

a. we, can   b. you, do   c. he, am   d. you, can

A: ___ **3.** He ___ comic books.

a. read   b. reading   c. see   d. reads

A: ___ **4.** "I think I can find a cheaper price. I'm going to ___ around."

a. buy   b. play   c. shop   d. cost

A: ___ **5.** How ___ pizza is there? There is ___ pizza.

a. many, big   b. much, a lot of   c. small, many   d. much, all

A: ___ **6.** Is ___ a lot of coffee? No, ___ isn't.

a. there, there   b. this, lot   c. them, she   d. it, he

A: ___ **7.** My grandmother ___ a lot of soda.

a. want   b. wanting   c. wants   d. doesn't

A: ___ **8.** "I need that job to put ___ on the table."

a. food   b. money   c. meat   d. milk

A: ___ **9.** What ___ you want? I don't ___ a banana.

a. do, try   b. can't, want   c. can, have   d. don't, want

A: ___ **10.** ___ there seven cherries? No, there ___.

a. Is, isn't   b. Our, aren't   c. Are, aren't   d. Have, hasn't

A: ___ **11.** We ___ eight pineapples.

a. needing   b. needs   c. need   d. is need

A: ___ **12.** "He's not a nice guy. He's really a bad ___."

a. tomato   b. orange   c. lemon   d. apple

A: ___ **13.** What color is ___ oval? That ___ a purple oval.

a. that, is   b. this, are   c. an, can   d. purple, has

A: ___ **14.** Is this ___ blue? Yes, it ___.

a. circle, can   b. heart, does   c. square, is   d. star, blue

A: ___ **15.** I can't ___ an orange octagon.

a. finding   b. found   c. find   d. be found

A: ___ **16.** "He really needs to get healthy. He's really ___ shape."

a. into   b. taking   c. losing   d. out of

Answers on page 206

Lesson 13: At the supermarket

в супермаркете

What do you want to buy?

I want to buy some bread.

Section A — Words

1. **milk**
   молоко
2. **juice**
   сок
3. **meat**
   мясо
4. **drinks**
   напитки
5. **vegetables**
   овощи

6. **ice cream**
   мороженое
7. **fruit**
   фрукт
8. **bread**
   хлеб
9. **fish**
   рыба
10. **pizza**
    пицца

Section B — Make a sentence

What do you want to buy?

I want to buy some <u>milk</u>.

What don't you want to buy?

I don't want to buy any <u>ice cream</u>.

Learn: some, any

Do you want to buy some <u>juice</u>?

Yes, I do. / No, I don't.

Do you want to buy some <u>fruit</u>?

Yes, I do. / No, I don't.

get – getting – got – gotten получать

I **get** my bread at the supermarket.

He is **getting** some bananas from the fruit market.

Last night, she **got** a pizza for dinner.

We haven't **gotten** any vegetables yet.

A rip off

Meaning: Something is too expensive.

"The supermarket around the corner is *a rip off*."

Trace and fill in the words

1. What do you want to buy?

I want to buy some fruit.

2. What don't you want _____ buy?

I don't want to buy any bread.

3. What _____ you want to _____?

I want to _____ some _____.

4. What _____ you _____ to buy?

I don't want to _____ any _____.

5. Do you want to buy some fish?

Yes, I _____.

6. Do you want to buy some milk?

No, I don't.

7. Do you _____ to buy _____ _____?

Yes, I _____.

8. Do you want to _____ some _____?

No, I _____.

At the supermarket!

Read the conversation

Max: What do you want to buy?

Julie: I want to buy some milk.

Max: What don't you want to buy?

Julie: I don't want to buy any meat.

Max: What do you want to buy?

Julie: I want to buy some fruit.

Max: What do you want to buy?

Julie: I want to buy some bread.

Max: What don't you want to buy?

Julie: I don't want to buy any fish.

Max: What do you want to buy?

Julie: I want to buy some vegetables.

Circle the things Julie wants

meat   milk   fruit   fish   vegetables

ice cream   bread   pizza   drinks   juice

Write the things she wants in the shopping cart

1._____
2._____
3._____
4._____

Lesson 14: At the ice cream shop

в магазине мороженого

Which flavor do you like?

I like mint flavor.

Section A — Words

1. **chocolate**
   шоколадное
2. **strawberry**
   клубничное
3. **mint**
   мятное
4. **raspberry**
   малиновое
5. **cherry**
   вишневое

6. **vanilla**
   ванильное
7. **coffee**
   кофейное
8. **almond**
   миндальное
9. **caramel**
   карамельное
10. **coconut**
    кокосовое

Section B — Make a sentence

Which flavor do you like?

I like <u>chocolate</u> flavor.

I don't like <u>almond</u> flavor.

Which flavor does he like?

He likes <u>vanilla</u> flavor.

He doesn't like <u>raspberry</u> flavor.

Do you like <u>strawberry</u> ice cream?

Yes, I do. / No, I don't.

Does she like <u>mint</u> ice cream?

Yes, she does. / No, she doesn't.

have/has – having – had – had иметь

She **has** coffee ice cream in her refrigerator.

I am **having** mint ice cream instead.

My sister **had** almond ice cream last time.

My father hasn't **had** caramel ice cream yet.

Flavor of the month

Meaning: Something is suddenly popular for a short time.

"This song is just the *flavor of the month*."

Trace and fill in the words

1. Which flavor do you like?

I like coconut flavor.

2. Which flavor does he like?

He _____ chocolate flavor.

3. Which _____ do you _____?

I like _____ _____.

4. Which _____ does she _____?

She _____ _____ _____.

5. Do you like vanilla ice cream?

No, I don't.

6. Does she like coffee ice cream?

Yes, she does.

7. Do you _____ _____ ice cream?

Yes, I _____.

8. Does he _____ _____ ice cream?

No, _____ _____.

At the ice cream shop!

don't   raspberry   do   like   you   flavor   she   does

1. Which _____ do you like? I _____ chocolate flavor.

2. Which flavor _____ you like? I like _____ flavor.

3. Which flavor _____ she like? _____ likes mint flavor.

4. Do _____ like vanilla flavor? No, I _____.

Do or Does?

1. What flavor _____ she like?

2. What flavor _____ they like?

3. What flavor _____ he like?

4. What flavor _____ you like?

5. _____ you like strawberry flavor?

6. _____ he like vanilla flavor?

7. _____ they like vanilla flavor?

8. _____ she like vanilla flavor?

9. Yes, they _____.

10. No, she _____ not.

Lesson 15: In the refrigerator

в холодильнике

> **What do you want to eat?**
> **I want to eat rice.**

1. **rice**
   рис
2. **salad**
   салад
3. **toast**
   тост
4. **soup**
   суп
5. **dumplings**
   пельмениа

6. **tea**
   чай
7. **cola**
   кола
8. **eggs**
   яйца
9. **water**
   вода
10. **ice**
    лед

Section B   Make a sentence

What do you want to <u>eat</u>?

I want to eat <u>rice</u>.

I don't want to eat <u>dumplings</u>.

What does he want to <u>drink</u>?

He wants to drink <u>tea</u>.

He doesn't want to drink <u>cola</u>.

Do you want to <u>eat</u> <u>salad</u>?

Yes, I do. / No, I don't.

Does she want to <u>drink</u> <u>juice</u>?

Yes, she does. / No, she doesn't.

sell – selling – sold – sold продавать

They **sell** eggs at the supermarket.

He was **selling** delicious dumplings at the market last night.

Last week, they **sold** me some cheap rice.

The supermarket has never **sold** ice.

Be as cold as ice

Meaning: To describe someone who is very unfriendly.

"The teacher *was as cold as ice* after she caught me cheating on the science test."

Trace and fill in the words

1. What do you want to drink?

I want to drink water.

2. What does he want to eat?

He _____ to eat soup.

3. What _____ you want to _____?

I want to eat _____.

4. What _____ she _____ to drink?

She wants to _____ _____.

5. Do you want to eat toast?

Yes, I do.

6. Does he _____ to drink tea?

No, he doesn't.

7. Do you _____ to drink _____?

Yes, I _____.

8. Does _____ want to eat _____?

No, she _____.

In the refrigerator!

1	2	3	4	5	6	7	8	9	10	11	12	13
a	b	c	d	e	f	g	h	i	j	k	l	m
14	15	16	17	18	19	20	21	22	23	24	25	26
n	o	p	q	r	s	t	u	v	w	x	y	z

Write the words using the code above

1. 19-15-21-16 __ __ __ __   **2.** 20-15-1-19-20 __ __ __ __ __

3. 19-1-12-1-4 __ __ __ __ __   **4.** 18-9-3-5 __ __ __ __

5. 23-1-20-5-18 __ __ __ __ __   **6.** 3-15-12-1 __ __ __ __

This man's refigerator has no food!
Help him write a shopping list!

Shopping list

1. _____dumplings_____
2. _____
3. _____
4. _____
5. _____
6. _____
7. _____
8. _____

Lesson 16: Jobs

работа

> **What is her job?**
> **She is a salesclerk.**

Section A   Words

1. **doctor**
   врач
2. **cook**
   повар
3. **nurse**
   медсестра, медбрат
4. **police officer**
   полицейский
5. **taxi driver**
   таксист

6. **teacher**
   учитель
7. **farmer**
   фермер
8. **salesclerk**
   продавец
9. **firefighter**
   пожарный
10. **builder**
    строитель

Section B Make a sentence

What is her job?

She is a <u>doctor</u>.

She isn't a <u>nurse</u>.

What is his job?

He is a <u>teacher</u>.

He isn't a <u>salesclerk</u>.

Is he a <u>farmer</u>?

Yes, he is. / No, he isn't.

Are they <u>teacher</u>s?

Yes, they are. / No, they aren't.

work – working – worked – worked работать

I **work** on a farm every day.

She wasn't **working** at the hospital last year.

My mother **worked** at the police station yesterday.

He hasn't **worked** for two years.

Keep up the good work

Meaning: To encourage someone to keep doing well.

"You're doing a great job. *Keep up the good work*."

Trace and fill in the words

1. What is his job?

He is a cook.

2. What is _____ job?

She is a teacher.

3. What _____ his _____?

_____ is a _____.

4. What is _____ job?

She _____ a _____.

5. Is she a builder?

No, she isn't.

6. Are they doctors?

No, they aren't.

7. Is _____ a _____?

Yes, she _____.

8. Are we _____?

Yes, _____ _____.

Jobs!

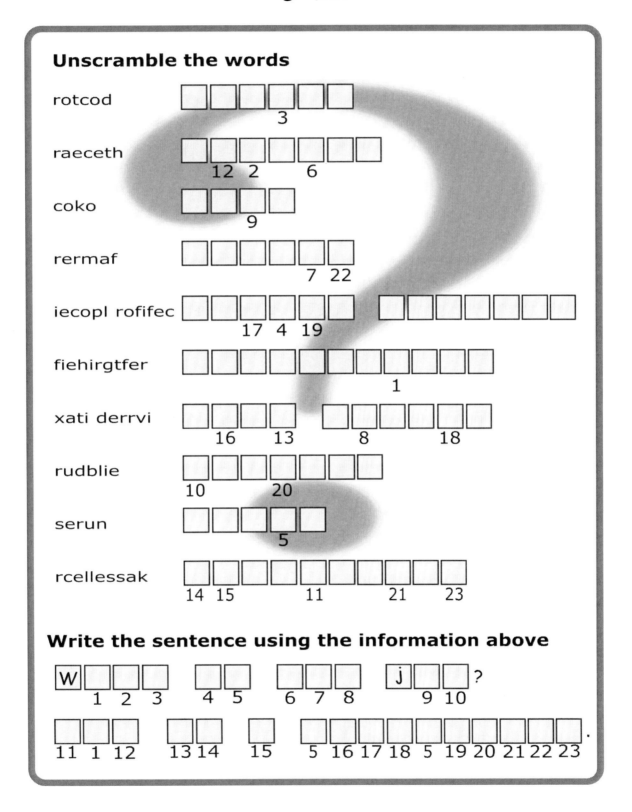

Unscramble the words

rotcod ☐☐☐☐☐☐
　　　　　　3

raeceth ☐☐☐☐☐☐☐
　　　　12 2　6

coko ☐☐☐☐
　　　　9

rermaf ☐☐☐☐☐☐
　　　　　7 22

iecopl rofifec ☐☐☐☐☐☐ ☐☐☐☐☐☐☐
　　　　　17 4 19

fiehirgtfer ☐☐☐☐☐☐☐☐☐☐☐
　　　　　　　　1

xati derrvi ☐☐☐☐ ☐☐☐☐☐
　　　　16　13　　8　　18

rudblie ☐☐☐☐☐☐☐
　　　10　　20

serun ☐☐☐☐☐
　　　5

rcellessak ☐☐☐☐☐☐☐☐☐☐
　　14 15　　11　　21　23

Write the sentence using the information above

W	☐	☐	☐		☐	☐		☐	☐	☐		j	☐	☐	?
	1	2	3		4	5		6	7	8			9	10	

☐☐☐　☐☐　☐　☐☐☐☐☐☐☐☐☐☐ .
11 1 12　13 14　15　5 16 17 18 5 19 20 21 22 23

Write the answer next to the letter "A"

A: ___ **1.** What does he want to ___? He ___ to buy some milk.

a. buys, want   b. buy, have   c. buys, wants d. buy, wants

A: ___ **2.** Do you ___ to buy some ___? Yes, I do.

a. wants, meat   b. want, bread   c. want, apple   d. wants, drinks

A: ___ **3.** She ___ the vegetables at the supermarket.

a. get   b. getting   c. got   d. is get

A: ___ **4.** "That was too expensive. What a rip ___."

a. of   b. over   c. off   d. curl

A: ___ **5.** Which flavor ___ he like? He ___ mint flavor.

a. do, like   b. can, like   c. does, like   d. does, likes

A: ___ **6.** ___ you like chocolate ice cream? Yes, I ___.

a. Does, does   b. Can, does   c. Do, like   d. Do, do

A: ___ **7.** They didn't ___ almond ice cream.

a. have   b. has   c. having   d. had

A: ___ **8.** "That new book is just the ___ of the month."

a. taste   b. word   c. ice cream   d. flavor

A: ___ **9.** What ___ she want to drink? She wants to ___ cola.

a. do, try   b. does, drink   c. can, have   d. don't, want

A: ___ **10.** Do ___ want to eat salad? No, I ___.

a. he, doesn't b. you, don't   c. you, not like   d. we, haven't

A: ___ **11.** They are ___ coffee.

a. sell   b. sells   c. selling   d. sold

A: ___ **12.** "She wasn't friendly. She was as ___ as ice."

a. melted   b. cold   c. dry   d. mean

A: ___ **13.** What is ___ job? She ___ a taxi driver.

a. she, is   b. hers, can   c. she's, be   d. her, is

A: ___ **14.** ___ they teachers? No, they ___.

a. Are, don't   b. Do, don't   c. Have, haven't   d. Are, aren't

A: ___ **15.** They ___ at a school.

a. work   b. works   c. working   d. has worked

A: ___ **16.** "You're doing well. Keep ___ the good work."

a. into   b. on   c. going   d. up

Answers on page 206

Lesson 17: Names

имена

What's her name?

Her name is Helen.

Section A | Words

1. **John**
   Джон
2. **Matthew**
   Мэттью
3. **Jason**
   Джейсон
4. **Helen**
   Хелен
5. **Mary**
   Мэри

6. **Kevin**
   Кевин
7. **Tom**
   Том
8. **Emily**
   Эмили
9. **Jessica**
   Джессика
10. **Susan**
    Сьюзан

Section B | Make a sentence

What's <u>your</u> name?

My name is <u>John</u>.

What's <u>her</u> name?

Her name is <u>Susan</u>.

Learn: my, your, his, her

Note: What's = What is

Is <u>his</u> name <u>Jason</u>?

Yes, it is. / No, it isn't.

Is <u>her</u> name <u>Emily</u>?

Yes, it is. / No, it isn't.

call – calling – called – called звонить

You can **call** him Jason.

I will be **calling** you tomorrow at 9:30 A.M.

Kevin **called** Mary yesterday.

Helen hasn't **called** Matthew back yet.

A household name

Meaning: To describe someone famous who everyone knows.

"The actor became *a household name* after he won an Oscar for his performance."

Trace and fill in the words

1. What's your name?

My name is Susan.

2. What's his name?

His name _____ Tom.

3. What's _____ name?

My _____ is _____.

4. What's _____ _____?

Her name _____ _____.

5. Is his name John?

Yes, it is.

6. Is her name Jessica?

No, it isn't.

7. Is _____ name _____?

Yes, it _____.

8. Is _____ _____ Kevin?

No, _____ isn't.

Names!

Write their names

1. __ __ __ __

2. __ __ __

3. __ __ __ __ __

4. __ __ __ __

5. __ __ __ __ __

What's your name?

_____

Answer the questions

1. What is her name?

   Her name is Mary.

2. What is his name?

   _____

3. What is her name?

   _____

4. What is his name?

   _____

5. What is his name?

   _____

Lesson 18: More places

еще места

Where did you go yesterday?

I went to school.

Section A — Words

1. **the library**
   библиотека
2. **school**
   школа
3. **the hospital**
   больница
4. **the train station**
   железнодорожная станция
5. **the police station**
   полицейский участок
6. **the office**
   офис
7. **the factory**
   завод, фабрика
8. **the clinic**
   клиника
9. **the bus stop**
   автобусная остановка
10. **the fire station**
    пожарное депо

Section B — Make a sentence

Where did you go <u>yesterday</u>?

I went to <u>the library</u>.

Where did they go <u>last week</u>?

They went to <u>the office</u>.

Learn: yesterday, last week, last night, last month

Note: didn't = did not

Did she go to <u>school</u> <u>last night</u>?

Yes, she did. / No, she didn't.

Did you go to <u>the factory</u> <u>yesterday</u>?

Yes, I did. / No, I didn't.

go – going – went – gone идти, ходить

I will **go** to the library after school.

When I was **going** to the office, I saw my friend.

Matthew **went** to the clinic this morning.

Mary hasn't **gone** to school yet.

Heart is in the right place

Meaning: To mean well and try to do the right thing.

"He makes a lot of mistakes, but his *heart is in the right place*."

Trace and fill in the words

1. Where did you go yesterday?

I went to the police station.

2. Where _____ they go last night?

They went to _____ clinic.

3. Where _____ we _____ last week?

_____ went to the _____.

4. Where did _____ go _____?

She _____ to the _____.

5. Did he go to the bus stop yesterday?

Yes, he did.

6. Did you _____ to the train station last night?

No, I _____.

7. Did _____ go to the _____ last week?

Yes, _____ _____.

8. Did she _____ to the _____ last night?

No, _____ _____.

More places!

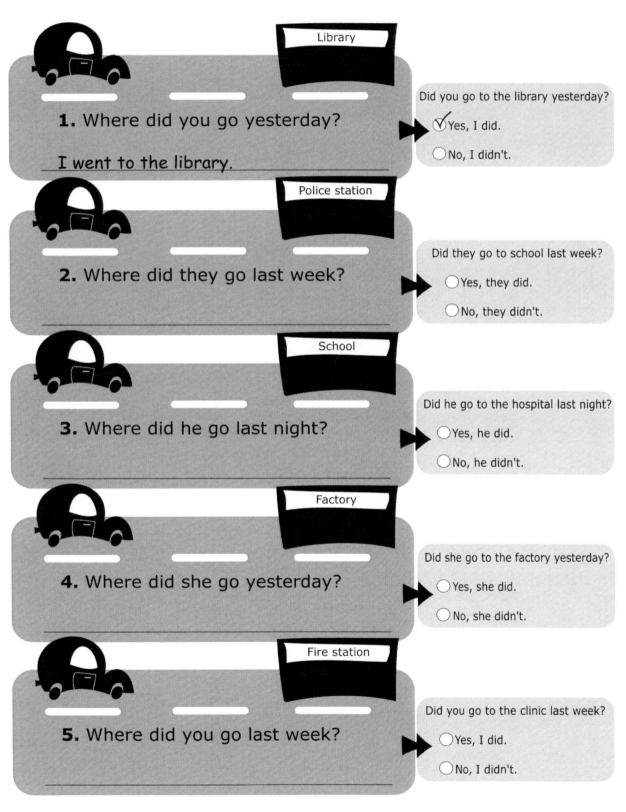

1. Where did you go yesterday?

I went to the library.

Library

Did you go to the library yesterday?
- ✓ Yes, I did.
- ○ No, I didn't.

2. Where did they go last week?

Police station

Did they go to school last week?
- ○ Yes, they did.
- ○ No, they didn't.

3. Where did he go last night?

School

Did he go to the hospital last night?
- ○ Yes, he did.
- ○ No, he didn't.

4. Where did she go yesterday?

Factory

Did she go to the factory yesterday?
- ○ Yes, she did.
- ○ No, she didn't.

5. Where did you go last week?

Fire station

Did you go to the clinic last week?
- ○ Yes, I did.
- ○ No, I didn't.

Lesson 19: Meats

мясо

> **What did he eat for lunch?**
>
> **He ate chicken.**

Section A — Words

1. **beef**
   говядина
2. **pork**
   свинина
3. **bacon**
   бекон
4. **fish**
   рыба
5. **salami**
   салями

6. **chicken**
   курица
7. **lamb**
   баранина
8. **ham**
   ветчина
9. **sausage**
   колбаса, сосиски
10. **shrimp**
    креветка

Section B — Make a sentence

What did he eat for <u>lunch</u>?

He ate <u>beef</u>.

He didn't eat <u>chicken</u>.

Learn: breakfast, lunch, dinner

Did they eat <u>ham</u> for <u>breakfast</u>?

Yes, they did. / No, they didn't.

Did you eat <u>fish</u> for <u>dinner</u>?

Yes, I did. / No, I didn't.

eat – eating – ate – eaten есть

I **eat** bacon for breakfast every Sunday.

They're not **eating** meat.

We **ate** a sandwich with cheese and salami yesterday.

I had never **eaten** German sausages until I went there.

Beef up

Meaning: To strengthen something or somebody.

"We need to *beef up* our efforts if we are going to do well this year."

Trace and fill in the words

1. What did she eat for lunch?

She ate ham. She didn't eat fish.

2. What did they eat for dinner?

They ate pork. They didn't _____ shrimp.

3. What _____ he eat _____ lunch?

_____ ate _____. He didn't _____ beef.

4. _____ did you _____ for breakfast?

I _____ fish. _____ didn't eat _____.

5. Did we eat sausage for lunch?

Yes, we _____.

6. Did you eat lamb for dinner?

No, I _____.

7. Did _____ eat _____ for lunch?

Yes, he _____.

8. Did they _____ bacon for _____?

No, _____ _____.

Meats!

Find the words!

```
f e p l x e m s x h e m d b o h z a l u
e p r n y l o q u y m x y r w g r p g d
i c r l y o i q d z m a u a p f q b s g
r v b k v y b n e z i x x q d r e c b h
r y u o r w l j g d s n z u u s l l z z
l h b e e f k w v q n b j e g f b w c m
c i b k b s q x b g m o i g n k n d r p
f q x b q a e k m f j o c b l s p k h n
m x j t o u n z z m f f s a l a m i y y
v i r m i a k e s k r g e k b u m z a e
w n p w n k q z r v h p h e s s n b l p
q o h n s t q u c n w u z l r a d f u v
a p s i g e l b o b q f x w s g n d e w
l b k p j c g n n c x o i z q e t e r i
s g n s x v w q l o x h k y k b q q y y
j k a x e h x a s z y p a c k r e v t r
j o w n g q v f i s h r i m p n o f m p
o a d h o b i e t h o h c q z n c p b m
y k o b m l v h v i c r q i k b c o f i
f i q a m x g l q k z w s n a w t n w w
```

~~beef~~   shrimp
pork   bacon
ham   sausage
fish   lamb
chicken   salami

Lesson 20: Vegetables

овощи

What will you cook tonight?
I will cook pumpkin.

Section A — Words

1. **pumpkin**
   тыква
2. **potato**
   картофель
3. **carrot**
   морковь
4. **asparagus**
   спаржа
5. **broccoli**
   брокколи

6. **corn**
   кукуруза
7. **cabbage**
   капуста
8. **spinach**
   шпинат
9. **mushroom**
   гриб
10. **onion**
    лук

Section B — Make a sentence

What will he cook <u>tonight</u>?

He will cook <u>pumpkin</u>.

What won't she cook <u>tomorrow</u>?

She won't cook <u>onion</u>.

Learn: tonight, tomorrow, later, next week

Note: won't = will not

Will we cook <u>carrot</u> <u>later</u>?

Yes, we will. / No, we won't.

Will you cook <u>asparagus</u> <u>tomorrow</u>?

Yes, I will. / No, I won't.

cook – cooking – cooked – cooked готовить пищу

She always **cooks** onions with the potatoes.

Mary will be **cooking** dinner for us tonight.

John **cooked** a delicious meal for us last weekend.

I've **cooked** cabbage and mushroom a lot lately.

Carrot on a stick

Meaning: A reward that is promised upon completion of a task.

"The coach gave his players a *carrot on a stick* and promised to take them all out for dinner if they win the game."

Trace and fill in the words

1. What will he cook tonight?

He will cook corn.

2. What won't she cook tomorrow?

She won't _____ spinach.

3. What _____ he _____ later?

_____ will _____ onion. He won't cook _____.

4. What will _____ cook tonight?

She _____ cook _____.

5. Will they cook carrot tomorrow?

Yes, they _____.

6. Will you cook asparagus tomorrow?

No, I _____.

7. Will she _____ mushroom _____?

Yes, _____ will.

8. Will _____ cook _____ tomorrow?

No, we _____.

Vegetables!

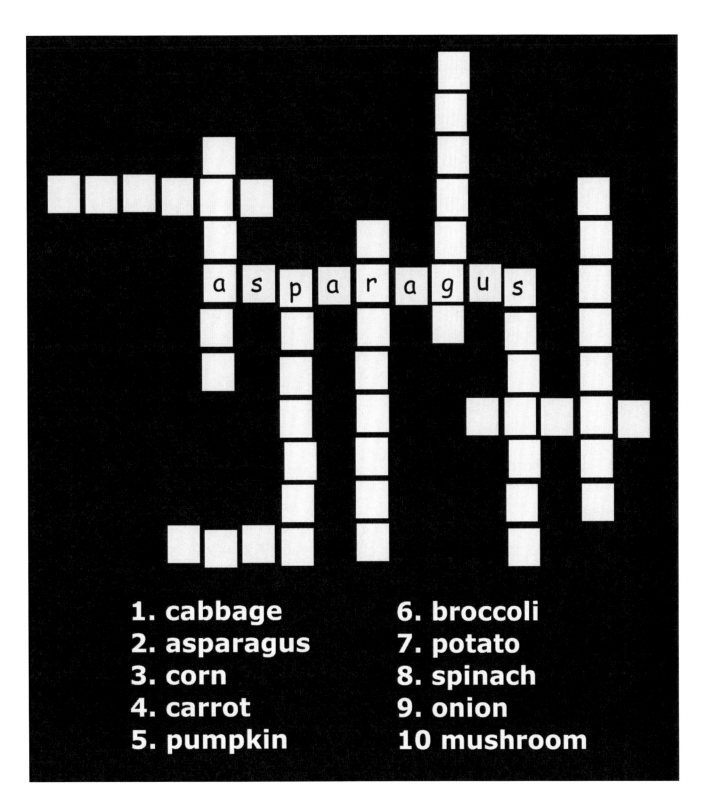

1. cabbage
2. asparagus
3. corn
4. carrot
5. pumpkin

6. broccoli
7. potato
8. spinach
9. onion
10 mushroom

Write the answer next to the letter "A"

A: ___ **1.** What's her ___? ___ name is Helen.

a. name, Her b. name, She's c. names, Her d. name, She

A: ___ **2.** ___ his name Kevin? Yes, ___ is.

a. Is, it b. Is, he c. Can, it d. Does, it

A: ___ **3.** Yesterday, Matthew ___ a green marker.

a. has b. is having c. had d. did had

A: ___ **4.** "She's really famous. She's a ___ name."

a. homely b. household c. real d. star

A: ___ **5.** Where ___ you go yesterday? I ___ to the clinic.

a. do, go b. did, go c. does, went d. did, went

A: ___ **6.** ___ she go to the office last night? Yes, she ___.

a. Does, go b. Can, does c. Did, goes d. Did, did

A: ___ **7.** I ___ to the train station every week.

a. gone b. go c. going d. goes

A: ___ **8.** "He means well. His ___ is in the right place."

a. heart b. words c. mind d. smile

A: ___ **9.** What ___ he eat for dinner? He ___ eat pork.

a. does, didn't   b. is, is   c. didn't, didn't   d. did, was

A: ___ **10.** ___ they eat sausage for lunch? No, they ___.

a. Were, weren't   b. Did, don't   c. Like, not like   d. Did, didn't

A: ___ **11.** She has ___ all of the ham.

a. eat   b. ate   c. eaten   d. eating

A: ___ **12.** "He wants to get stronger. He said he wants to beef ___."

a. out   b. up   c. on   d. in

A: ___ **13.** What ___ he cook later? He will ___ broccoli.

a. is, cook   b. will, cooks   c. has, cook   d. will, cook

A: ___ **14.** ___ we cook asparagus tonight? ___, we will.

a. Can, Can   b. Don't, Do   c. Will, Yes   d. Are, Yes

A: ___ **15.** She will ___ vegetables tomorrow.

a. cook   b. cooks   c. cooking   d. cooked

A: ___ **16.** "I think the reward is like a ___ on a stick."

a. potato   b. pumpkin   c. carrot   d. mushroom

Answers on page 206

Lesson 21: At school

в школе

> **Where is the art room?**
> **The art room is next to the gym.**

Section A	Words

1. **classroom**
   класс, классная комната
2. **office**
   офис, кабинет
3. **nurse's office**
   медпункт
4. **gym**
   спортзал
5. **hall**
   зал

6. **computer lab**
   компьютерный класс
7. **art room**
   класс искусств
8. **music room**
   музыкальный класс
9. **science lab**
   класс естественных наук
10. **lunchroom**
    столовая

Section B	Make a sentence

Where is the <u>classroom</u>?

The classroom is <u>across from</u> the <u>office</u>.

Where is the <u>computer lab</u>?

The computer lab is <u>between</u> the <u>gym</u> and the <u>hall</u>.

Learn: across from, next to, between

Is the <u>art room</u> <u>next to</u> the <u>music room</u>?

Yes, it is. / No, it's <u>next to</u> the <u>science lab</u>.

Is the <u>nurse's office</u> <u>next to</u> the <u>office</u>?

Yes, it is. / No, it's <u>across from</u> the <u>computer lab</u>.

put – putting – put – put ложить, ставить

You can **put** the guitar in the music room.

We are **putting** the chairs in the new office.

The students already **put** the books in the computer lab.

She hasn't **put** any food in the lunchroom yet.

Old school

Meaning: To do something the old-fashioned way.

"We're going to do this *old school* and use a hammer and nails."

Trace and fill in the words

1. Where is the office?

The office is next to the lunchroom.

2. Where _____ the gym?

The gym is _____ the art room and the science lab.

3. Where _____ the _____ room?

The music room is across from the _____.

4. _____ is the _____ lab?

The science lab is _____ the lunchroom and the _____.

5. Is the art room next to the music room?

Yes, it is.

6. Is the computer lab _____ to the hall?

No, it's _____ the gym and the art room.

7. _____ the nurse's office next to the _____?

Yes, it is.

8. Is the hall across _____ the classroom?

No, it's _____ the _____ and the office.

At school!

Answer the questions

1. Where is the gym?

   _____.

2. Where is the classroom?

   _____.

3. Where is the nurse's office?

   _____.

4. Is the lunchroom next to the hall?

   _____.

5. Is the science lab across from the office?

   _____.

Lesson 22: School subjects

школьные предметы

What class do you have after math?

I have an art class after math.

Words

1. **science**
   естественные науки
2. **English**
   английский язык
3. **P.E.**
   физкультура
4. **geography**
   география
5. **social studies**
   социология

6. **math**
   математика
7. **art**
   изобразительное искусство
8. **music**
   музыка
9. **history**
   история
10. **computer**
    компьютер

Section B Make a sentence

What class do you have <u>after</u> <u>science</u>?

I have a <u>geography</u> class after science.

What class does he have <u>before</u> <u>science</u>?

He has a <u>history</u> class before science.

Learn: after, before / have, has

Do you have a <u>math</u> class after <u>history</u>?

Yes, I do. / No, I have a <u>music</u> class.

Does he have a <u>math</u> class before <u>English</u>?

Yes, he does. / No, he has a <u>computer</u> class.

do – doing – did – done делать

He couldn't **do** most of the questions on the math test.

They are **doing** the science project now.

John **did** really well on his English test last semester.

I will have already **done** the history homework by Sunday.

Cut class

Meaning: To miss class on purpose.

"Jenny *cut class* after she realized she didn't do her math homework."

Trace and fill in the words

1. What class do you have after math?

I have an English class after math.

2. What class does she have before art?

She has a music _____ before art.

3. What _____ do you have _____ history?

I _____ a geography class before _____.

4. What class does _____ have after _____?

She _____ a science class _____ P.E.

5. Do you _____ a math class after history?

Yes, I _____.

6. Does he have a science _____ after English?

No, he _____ a computer class.

7. Do _____ have an art class before _____?

Yes, you _____.

8. Does _____ have a P.E. class _____ music?

No, she _____ an _____ class.

School Subjects!

I have a geography class after science.
I have an English class before science.
I have a math class before English.
I have a history class after geography.
I have a computer class before math.

Fill out the School Schedule using the information above

School Schedule

9am _____

10am _____

11am _____

1pm science class

2pm _____

3pm _____

True or False? Circle the answer

1. You have a science class before geography. **True**   **False**

2. You have a computer class after math. **True**   **False**

3. You have a history class after geography. **True**   **False**

4. You have an English class after science. **True**   **False**

Lesson 23: Chores

работа по дому

> **What do you need to do today?**
> **I need to feed the pets.**

Section A	Words

1. wash the dishes
помыть посуду

2. feed the pets
покормить животных

3. vacuum the carpet
почистить пылесосом ковер

4. take out the trash
вынести мусор

5. clean the bedroom
сделать уборку в спальне

6. mop the floor
вытереть пол

7. cook dinner
приготовить ужин

8. do the laundry
постирать одежду

9. iron the clothes
погладить одежду

10. make the beds
заправить постель

Section B	Make a sentence

What do you need to do <u>this morning</u>?

This morning, I need to <u>wash the dishes</u>.

What does he need to do <u>this afternoon</u>?

This afternoon, he needs to <u>mop the floor</u>.

Learn: this morning, this afternoon, this evening, today

Do you need to <u>make the beds</u> <u>this morning</u>?

Yes, I do. / No, I don't.

Does he need to <u>iron the clothes</u> <u>this afternoon</u>?

Yes, he does. / No, he doesn't.

know – knowing – knew – known знать

I don't **know** what to feed the pets.

There is no way of **knowing** which chores have been done.

Mary **knew** the trash hadn't been taken out yet.

I hadn't **known** at the time that nobody did the laundry.

All in a day's work

Meaning: A normal day without a change in routine.

"Taking out the trash before school is *all in a day's work*."

Trace and fill in the words

1. What do you need to do this afternoon?

This afternoon, I need to do the laundry.

2. What does he _____ to do this morning?

This morning, he _____ to make the beds.

3. _____ do you need to do this _____?

This afternoon, _____ need to feed the _____.

4. What _____ she _____ to do today?

Today, _____ needs to do the _____.

5. Do you need to iron the clothes this evening?

Yes, I _____.

6. Does he need to _____ the beds this morning?

No, he _____.

7. Do _____ need to _____ the carpet today?

No, I _____.

8. Does she need to cook _____ this evening?

Yes, she _____.

Section G	Let's have fun

Chores!

Connect the sentences

What do you need to do this morning? •   • This morning, she needs to do the dishes.

                                               • This morning, I need to wash the clothes.
What does he need to do this afternoon? •

What does she need to do this morning? •   • This evening, they need to cook dinner.

What do they need to do this evening? •   • This afternoon, we need to make the beds.

What do we need to do this afternoon? •   • This afternoon, he needs to feed the pets.

Unscramble the sentences

wash the / morning / need to / I / this / dishes

1. _____ .

she / the pets / needs to / this afternoon / feed

2. _____ .

to / the laundry / need / they / do / this evening

3. _____ .

this afternoon / the trash / he / needs to / take out

4. _____ .

Lesson 24: At the toy store

в магазине игрушек

What are you playing with?

I'm playing with my ball.

Section A	Words

1. **doll**
   кукла
2. **teddy bear**
   игрушечный медведь
3. **car**
   автомобиль
4. **airplane**
   самолет
5. **dinosaur**
   динозавр

6. **robot**
   робот
7. **ball**
   мяч
8. **jump rope**
   скакалка
9. **board game**
   настольная игра
10. **blocks**
    кубики

Section B	Make a sentence

What are you playing with?

I am playing with <u>my</u> <u>doll</u>.

What is he playing with?

He is playing with <u>his</u> <u>robot</u>.

Learn: my, your, his, her, their, our, its

Note: I'm = I am

Are you playing with <u>your</u> <u>teddy bear</u>?

Yes, I am. / No, I'm not.

Is she playing with <u>her</u> <u>ball</u>?

Yes, she is. / No, she isn't.

borrow – borrowing – borrowed – borrowed одалживать

You can **borrow** my ball.

She will be **borrowing** the board game for tonight.

I **borrowed** a book about cars from the library yesterday.

They haven't **borrowed** these books yet.

Like a kid with a new toy

Meaning: To be really happy with something.

"He was *like a kid with a new toy* when he drove the car for the first time."

Trace and fill in the words

1. What are you playing with?

I am playing with my teddy bear.

2. What is she playing _____?

She _____ playing with her ball.

3. What are _____ playing _____?

We _____ _____ with our board game.

4. What is he _____ with?

_____ is playing with his _____.

5. Are you playing _____ your car?

Yes, I am.

6. Is he playing with _____ airplane?

No, he isn't.

7. _____ you _____ with your jump rope?

_____, I'm _____.

8. _____ she playing _____ her dinosaur?

Yes, _____ _____.

Toys!

Circle the toys

1.   cool   geography   bag   (doll)   sister

2.   desk   blocks   math   father   milk

3.   teddy bear   history   classroom   beef

4.   pen   science   water   ball   gym

Write the word

1.

2.

3.

4.

Write the answer using the information above

1. What is she playing with? _____.

2. What is he playing with? _____.

3. Is she playing with her teddy bear? _____.

4. Is he playing with his robot? _____.

Write the answer next to the letter "A"

A: ___ **1.** ___ is the office? It's ___ to the gym.

a. There, next   b. Where, next   c. How, near   d. This, next

A: ___ **2.** ___ the hall across from the office? Yes, ___ is.

a. Does, it   b. Is, it   c. Are, they   d. Can, he

A: ___ **3.** They will ___ the art room later.

a. find   b. found   c. finding   d. finds

A: ___ **4.** "We did it the old-fashioned way. We did it old ___."

a. way   b. time   c. man   d. school

A: ___ **5.** What class ___ you ___ after science?

a. are, have   b. does, has   c. do, have   d. can, has

A: ___ **6.** ___ we have math class after art? Yes, we ___.

a. Can, are   b. Does, do   c. Do, do   d. Are, are

A: ___ **7.** They ___ gym class earlier today.

a. has   b. having   c. are had   d. had

A: ___ **8.** "She ___ class because she didn't do her homework".

a. put   b. cut   c. lost   d. made

A: ___ **9.** This morning, I ___ to ___ the pets.

a. need, feed   b. am, take   c. can, walk   d. need, make

A: ___ **10.** ___ we need to ___ the beds this morning?

a. Does, take   b. Are, open   c. Do, mop   d. Do, make

A: ___ **11.** He ___ to do the laundry before lunch.

a. needs   b. need   c. needing   d. is need

A: ___ **12.** "Cleaning the room after school is all in a day's ___."

a. time   b. work   c. travel   d. test

A: ___ **13.** What are you ___ with? I'm playing ___ my robot.

a. play, with   b. playing, with   c. plays, by   d. play, on

A: ___ **14.** Is he playing with ___ jump rope? Yes, he ___.

a. him, can   b. he, is   c. his, is   d. him, has

A: ___ **15.** She doesn't like to ___ with dinosaurs.

a. plays   b. playing   c. play   d. played

A: ___ **16.** "He was so happy, he was like a kid with a new ___."

a. car   b. bike   c. toy   d. ball

Answers on page 206

Lesson 25: In the Kitchen

в кухне

What was he cleaning?

He was cleaning the stove.

1. **refrigerator**
   холодильник
2. **coffee maker**
   кофеварка
3. **microwave oven**
   микроволновая печь
4. **stove**
   плита
5. **blender**
   блендер

6. **cupboard**
   кухонный шкаф
7. **rice cooker**
   рисоварка
8. **dish rack**
   сушилка для посуды
9. **pan**
   сковорода
10. **toaster**
    тостер

Section B   Make a sentence

What was he cleaning?

He was cleaning the <u>refrigerator</u>.

What were they claning?

They were cleaning the <u>cupboard</u>.

Note: weren't = were not, wasn't = was not

Was she cleaning the <u>coffee maker</u>?

Yes, she was. / No, she wasn't.

Were they cleaning the <u>toaster</u>?

Yes, they were. / No, they weren't.

clean – cleaning – cleaned – cleaned чистить, убирать

He **cleans** the gas stove every day.

We are **cleaning** the refrigerator.

My mother **cleaned** the toaster this morning.

I've already **cleaned** the blender, so you can use it now.

Too many cooks in the kitchen

Meaning: When too many people try to take control.

"We couldn't find a solution because there were *too many cooks in the kitchen*."

Trace and fill in the words

1. What was she cleaning?

She was cleaning the cupboard.

2. What were they cleaning?

They were _____ the coffee maker.

3. What _____ he cleaning?

_____ was _____ the pan.

4. _____ were _____ cleaning?

They _____ cleaning the toaster.

5. Was he cleaning the microwave oven?

No, he wasn't.

6. Were we cleaning the gas stove?

No, we _____.

7. Was _____ cleaning the _____?

Yes, she _____.

8. _____ they _____ the blender?

Yes, _____ _____.

In the Kitchen!

Write the missing words

| wasn't | was | you | were | pan | cleaning | she | the |

1. What _____ he cleaning? He was _____ the microwave.

2. What _____ they cleaning? They were cleaning _____ stove.

3. What was _____ cleaning? She was cleaning the _____.

4. Were _____ cleaning the blender? No, I _____.

Was or Were?

1. What _____ she cleaning?

She _____ cleaning the blender.

2. What _____ they cleaning?

They _____ cleaning the toaster.

3. What _____ you cleaning?

I _____ cleaning the refrigerator.

4. _____ he cleaning the cupboard?

Yes, he _____.

5. _____ they cleaning the rice cooker?

No, they _____ not.

Lesson 26: In the toolbox

в ящике для инструментов

What were you using to fix the chair?

I was using the electric drill.

1. **hammer**
молоток
2. **electric drill**
электродрель
3. **screwdriver**
отвертка
4. **paintbrush**
кисть
5. **shovel**
лопата

6. **tape measure**
рулетка
7. **axe**
топор
8. **pliers**
плоскогубцы
9. **ladder**
стремянка
10. **wrench**
ключ

Section B   Make a sentence

What were you using to fix the <u>table</u>?

I was using the <u>hammer</u>.

What was she using to fix the <u>fence</u>?

She was using the <u>pliers</u>.

Learn: table, chair, fence, roof, door, cupboard

Was he using the <u>electric drill</u> to <u>fix the chair</u>?

Yes, he was. / No, he wasn't.

Were they using the <u>ladder</u> to <u>fix the roof</u>?

Yes, they were. / No, they weren't.

use – using – used – used использовать

She **uses** the shovel to do the gardening.

They were **using** the wrench last week.

My father **used** the screwdriver earlier today.

My brother has never **used** an electric drill.

Tools of the trade

Meaning: Things that are needed for a specific job.

"My cell phone, diary and calculator are all *tools of the trade*."

Trace and fill in the words

1. What were you using to fix the table?

I was using the electric drill.

2. What was she _____ to fix the chair?

She _____ using the screwdriver.

3. What _____ you _____ to fix the door?

_____ was using the _____.

4. What was _____ using to _____ the roof?

He _____ _____ the ladder.

5. Was she using the pliers to fix the cupboard?

No, she wasn't.

6. Were they using the shovel to fix the fence?

No, _____ weren't.

7. Was _____ using the pliers to fix the _____?

Yes, he _____.

8. Were you using the hammer to fix the chair?

Yes, _____ _____.

In the toolbox!

Was or Were?

He _____ using the electric drill to fix the cupboard.

She _____ using the hammer to fix the fence.

They _____ using the tape measure to fix the door.

We _____ using the ladder to fix the roof.

I _____ using the pliers to fix the table.

John _____ using the screwdriver to fix the chair.

What was fixed?

1. _____   4. _____

2. _____   5. _____

3. _____   6. _____

Which tools weren't used?

1. _____

2. _____

3. _____

4. _____

Lesson 27: Transportation

транспорт

How will you be going to Rome?

I will be taking a bus.

Section A	Words

1. catch a bus
   сесть на автобус
2. take a taxi
   взять такси
3. take a ferry
   сесть на паром
4. ride a motorcycle
   водить мотоцикл
5. take the subway
   поехать на метро

6. take a train
   сесть на поезд
7. drive a car
   водить машину
8. ride a scooter
   водить скутер
9. ride a bicycle
   ехать на велосипеде
10. take an airplane
   полететь на самолете

Section B	Make a sentence

How will you be going to <u>New York</u>?

I will be <u>catching a bus</u> there.

Learn: New York, Sydney, Vancouver, Rome, London, Shanghai, Hong Kong, Paris, Berlin, Cape town, Buenos Aires, Venice

Note: I'll = I will

Will you be <u>taking a ferry</u> to <u>Hong Kong</u>?

Yes, I will be. / No, I'll be <u>taking an airplane</u>.

Will you be <u>riding a bicycle</u> to <u>Sydney</u>?

Yes, I will be. / No, I'll be <u>catching a bus</u>.

take – taking – took – taken брать

You can **take** the subway to work.

She will be **taking** a taxi to the restaurant.

We **took** a ferry to the Hong Kong airport last year.

I hadn't **taken** an airplane until I went to Rome.

Lose one's train of thought

Meaning: To forget what you were thinking about.

"I'm sorry, I *lost my train of thought*. What were we talking about?"

Trace and fill in the words

1. How will you be going to Sydney?

I will be taking a train there.

2. How will he be _____ to Vancouver?

He will _____ driving a car.

3. How _____ we be going to Rome?

_____ will be _____ a scooter there.

4. How will _____ be _____ to Paris?

They _____ be _____ an airplane.

5. Will you be riding a motorcycle to Berlin?

No, I'll be riding a bicycle.

6. Will _____ be _____ a ferry to Hong Kong?

No, they'll be taking an airplane.

7. Will _____ be _____ the subway to Venice?

No, he'll _____ catching a bus.

8. Will she _____ _____ a train to London?

Yes, _____ _____ _____.

Transportation!

Unscramble the words and write

1. | owh | illw | seh | eb | nggio | ot | enw | royk |

____ ____ ____ ____ ____ ____ ____ ____?

| hes | liwl | eb | katngi | a | riant | herte |

____ ____ ____ ____ ____ ____ ____.

2. | lwil | ouy | eb | dirngiv | a | rca | ot | omer |

____ ____ ____ ____ ____ ____ ____ ____?

| on | lil' | eb | atcihcgn | a | sbu | herte |

____ , ____ ____ ____ ____ ____ ____.

Connect the words

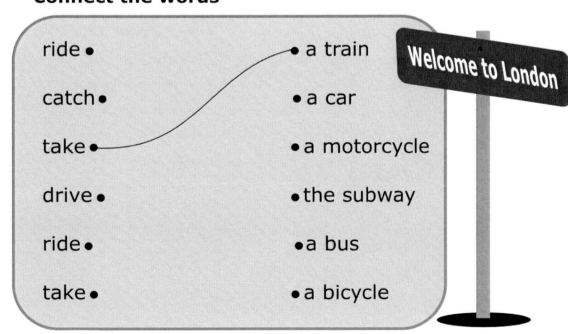

ride • • a train
catch • • a car
take • • a motorcycle
drive • • the subway
ride • • a bus
take • • a bicycle

Welcome to London

Lesson 28: Clothes

одежда

Whose jacket is that?

It's mine.

Section A	Words

1. T-shirt
футболка
2. blouse
блузка
3. scarf
шарф
4. coat
пальто
5. dress
платье

6. hat
шапка
7. sweater
свитер
8. jacket
куртка, пиджак
9. skirt
юбка
10. necktie
галстук

Section B	Make a sentence

Whose <u>T-shirt</u> is this?

It's <u>mine</u>.

Whose <u>hat</u> is that?

It's <u>yours</u>.

Learn: mine, yours, his, hers, theirs, ours

Is this your <u>sweater</u>?

Yes, it is. / No, it isn't.

Is this her <u>blouse</u>?

Yes, it is. / No, it isn't.

wear – wearing – wore – worn носить

You should **wear** a jacket today.

I don't like **wearing** a necktie.

She **wore** a skirt to school yesterday.

My sister hasn't **worn** a dress for a long time.

Wear somebody out

Meaning: To make someone tired.

"My boss completely *wore me out* today."

Trace and fill in the words

1. Whose hat is this?

It's mine.

2. Whose blouse _____ that?

It's hers.

3. Whose sweater _____ this?

_____ his.

4. _____ scarf _____ that?

_____ ours.

5. Is this your jacket?

No, _____ isn't.

6. Is this your coat?

_____, it is.

7. _____ this his jacket?

No, _____ _____.

8. _____ that her _____?

Yes, _____ _____.

Clothes!

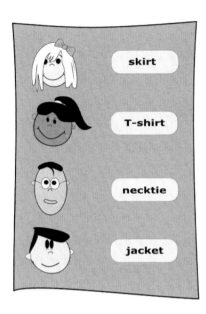

skirt

T-shirt

necktie

jacket

Write the answer

1. Whose skirt is this? _____.

2. Whose T-shirt is that? _____.

3. Whose necktie is this? _____.

4. Whose jacket is that? _____.

Complete the words

j__ck__t

bl__u__e

__o__t

sk__r__

d__e__s

swe__t__r

n__c__t__e

Is or Are?

1. _____ this your sweater?

Yes, it _____.

2. _____ that her T-shirt?

No, it _____ not.

3. _____ these his shoes?

Yes, they _____.

4. _____ those their jackets?

No, they _____ not.

Write the answer next to the letter "A"

A: ___ **1.** What ___ he cleaning? He was ___ the blender.

a. is, clean   b. can, cleans   c. was, cleaning   d. is, cleaned

A: ___ **2.** ___ they cleaning the cupboard? Yes, ___ were.

a. Are, we   b. Can, there   c. Were, they   d. Do, they

A: ___ **3.** They ___ the stove yesterday morning.

a. clean   b. cleaned   c. cleans   d. is cleaning

A: ___ **4.** "It's difficult because there are too many ___ in the kitchen."

a. cooks   b. cook   c. cooking   d. cooked

A: ___ **5.** She was ___ a hammer to fix the fence.

a. use   b. using   c. uses   d. used

A: ___ **6.** Was he ___ the axe to fix the tree? No, he ___.

a. using, wasn't   b. use, can't   c. uses, doesn't   d. used, isn't

A: ___ **7.** He ___ the pliers every Thursday.

a. use   b. using   c. uses   d. was use

A: ___ **8.** "These important things are all my ___ of the trade."

a. work   b. stuff   c. jobs   d. tools

A: ___ **9.** How will he be ___ to New York?

a. go   b. goes   c. went   d. going

A: ___ **10.** ___ you be ___ a taxi to Sydney? Yes, I will be.

a. Can, take   b. Are, riding   c. Will, taking   d. Do, takes

A: ___ **11.** They ___ a ferry to Hong Kong last night.

a. took   b. taken   c. taking   d. takes

A: ___ **12.** "I wasn't thinking clearly, I lost my ___ of thought."

a. taxi   b. mind   c. train   d. take

A: ___ **13.** ___ blouse is this? It's ___.

a. Who, my   b. Whose, mine   c. Wear, on   d. Who is, my

A: ___ **14.** Is that ___ jacket? Yes, ___ is.

a. she, it   b. her, it   c. him, this   d. his, they

A: ___ **15.** She was ___ a skirt at school yesterday.

a. wear   b. wore   c. wears   d. wearing

A: ___ **16.** "Doing my homework was tiring. It wore me ___."

a. over   b. on   c. in   d. out

Answers on page 206

Lesson 29: More clothes

ещё одежда

Section A	Words

1. **pants**
   брюки
2. **shorts**
   шорты
3. **shoes**
   туфли, ботинки
4. **dresses**
   платья
5. **shirts**
   рубашки

6. **jeans**
   джинсы
7. **socks**
   носки
8. **gloves**
   перчатки
9. **pajamas**
   пижамы
10. **boots**
    сапоги

Section B	Make a sentence

Whose <u>pants</u> are these?

They're <u>mine</u>.

Whose <u>jeans</u> are those?

They're <u>hers</u>.

Note: They're = They are

Are these <u>shoes</u> <u>yours</u>?

Yes, they are. / No, they aren't.

Are those <u>socks</u> <u>his</u>?

Yes, they are. / No, they aren't.

lend – lending – lent – lent давать в долг

I will **lend** my shirt to you.

He is **lending** me his gloves.

My mother **lent** her eraser to me.

I have **lent** my shovel to him before.

Fits like a glove

Meaning: Something is the right size.

"The new shirt you bought me *fits like a glove*."

Trace and fill in the words

1. Whose jeans are these?

They're mine.

2. Whose shorts _____ those?

_____ hers.

3. Whose socks are _____?

_____ his.

4. _____ shoes _____ those?

_____ hers.

5. Are these gloves yours?

No, they aren't.

6. _____ _____ dresses hers?

_____, they _____.

7. _____ _____ bags his?

Yes, _____ _____.

8. _____ those _____ mine?

No, _____ _____.

More clothes!

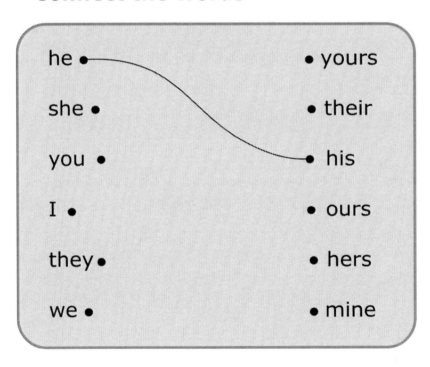

Write the answer

1. Whose dresses are those? _____.

2. Whose pants are these? _____.

3. Whose skirts are those? _____.

4. Whose shoes are these? _____.

Connect the words

he •   • yours
she •   • their
you •   • his
I •   • ours
they •   • hers
we •   • mine

Complete the words

p___ nts

sh___rt___

s___o___s

sk___rt

dre___s___s

g___ov___s

bo___ts

Lesson 30: In the living room

в гостиной

Where is the coffee table?

It's in front of the sofa.

Section A   Words

1. **bookcase**
   книжный шкаф
2. **television**
   телевизор
3. **clock**
   часы
4. **coffee table**
   кофейный столик
5. **armchair**
   кресло

6. **painting**
   картина
7. **TV stand**
   тумба для телевизора
8. **rug**
   ковер
9. **sofa**
   диван
10. **vase**
    ваза

Section B   Make a sentence

Where is the <u>bookcase</u>?

It's <u>next to</u> the <u>sofa</u>.

Where are the <u>books</u>?

They're <u>under</u> the <u>vase</u>.

Learn: in front of, behind, next to, on, under

Is there a <u>vase</u> on the <u>coffee table</u>?

Yes, there is. / No, there isn't.

Are there <u>pens</u> behind the <u>TV stand</u>?

Yes, there are. / No, there aren't.

move – moving – moved – moved двигаться

After dinner, I will **move** the coffee table.

They are **moving** the armchair next to the sofa.

Dad **moved** the television to the bedroom last night.

We still haven't **moved** the bookcase to the living room.

A race against the clock

Meaning: To not have too much time left to complete a task.

"It's *a race against the clock* to finish this project."

Trace and fill in the words

1. Where is the television?

It's in front of the sofa.

2. Where _____ the paintings?

They're next _____ the armchair.

3. _____ is the _____?

_____ behind the _____.

4. _____ _____ the vases?

_____ in front of the _____.

5. Is there a cup on the bookcase?

No, there isn't.

6. Are _____ pencils on the coffee table?

No, there aren't.

7. _____ _____ a notebook on the _____?

Yes, _____ _____.

8. _____ _____ books _____ the rug?

Yes, _____ _____.

In the living room!

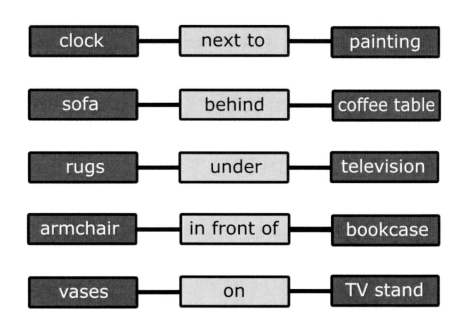

clock	next to	painting
sofa	behind	coffee table
rugs	under	television
armchair	in front of	bookcase
vases	on	TV stand

Choose the correct answer

Answer the questions

1. Where is the clock?

_____.

2. Where is the sofa?

_____.

3. Where are the rugs?

_____.

4. Where is the armchair?

_____.

5. Where are the vases?

_____.

1. Is there a clock next to the painting?

✓ Yes, there is.   ○ No, there isn't.

2. Is there a sofa behind the coffee table?

○ Yes, there is.   ○ No, there isn't.

3. Are there rugs under the bookcase?

○ Yes, there are.   ○ No, there aren't.

4. Is there an armchair in front of the sofa?

○ Yes, there is.   ○ No, there isn't.

5. Are there vases on the TV stand?

○ Yes, there are.   ○ No, there aren't.

Lesson 31: In the bathroom

В ванной комнате

What is above the sink?

There is a mirror above the sink.

Section A — Words

1. **mirror**
   зеркало
2. **bath towel**
   банное полотенце
3. **shower**
   душ
4. **toilet paper**
   туалетная бумага
5. **bath mat**
   коврик для ванной

6. **shelf**
   полка
7. **sink**
   мойка
8. **toilet**
   унитаз
9. **bathtub**
   ванна
10. **soap**
    мыло

Section B — Make a sentence

What is <u>beside</u> the <u>bathtub</u>?

There is a <u>bath mat</u> beside the bathtub.

What are <u>on</u> the <u>shelf</u>?

There are some <u>towel</u>s on the shelf.

There isn't any <u>toilet paper</u> in the bathroom.

There aren't any <u>bath towels</u> in the bathroom.

Is there a <u>shelf</u> <u>below</u> the <u>mirror</u>?

Yes, there is. / No, there isn't.

Is there <u>toilet paper</u> <u>beside</u> the <u>toilet</u>?

Yes, there is. / No, there isn't.

wash – washing – washed – washed мыть

She **washes** the sink every day.

He was **washing** his hands with the new soap.

Kevin **washed** the bath towel this morning.

I won't have **washed** the bath mat by tomorrow.

Throw in the towel

Meaning: To give up or quit.

"After trying three times, he decided to *throw in the towel*."

Trace and fill in the words

1. What is below the mirror?

There is a sink below the mirror.

2. What _____ beside the bath mat?

There is a bathtub _____ the bath mat.

3. _____ is _____ the toilet?

There _____ a shelf beside the _____ .

4. What _____ above _____ shower?

_____ is a shelf _____ the _____ .

5. Is there a showerhead above the bathtub?

No, _____ isn't.

6. Is there a mirror above _____ toilet?

Yes, there is.

7. Is _____ a bath towel next to the _____ ?

_____ , _____ isn't.

8. _____ _____ a sink beside the _____ ?

_____ , _____ is.

In the bathroom!

There is a mirror above the sink.
There are some bath towels on the shelf.
There aren't any towels in the bathroom.
There is a toilet beside the bathtub.
There isn't any soap in the bathroom.
There is a bath mat under the sink.

Read the information above. Choose the correct answer

1. Is there a mirror above the sink?   ☑Yes, there is   ○No, there isn't

2. Are there bath towels on the shelf?   ○Yes, there are   ○ No, there aren't

3. Are there any towels in the bathroom?   ○Yes, there are   ○ No, there aren't

4. Is there a toilet beside the bathtub?   ○Yes, there is   ○No, there isn't

5. Is there any soap in the bathroom?   ○Yes, there is   ○No, there isn't

6. Is there a bath mat under the sink?   ○Yes, there is   ○No, there isn't

Complete the words

m__rr __r   t__il __t

b__th__ub   to__l__t p__per

s__ow__r   sh__l__

s__a__   b__t__ to__el

s__n__   ba__h m__t

Lesson 32: In the bedroom

в спальне

What is on the left of the bed?
There is a lamp on the left of the bed.

Section A — Words

1. **bed**
   кровать
2. **pillow**
   подушка
3. **mattress**
   матрас
4. **blanket**
   одеяло
5. **drawers**
   комод

6. **lamp**
   лампа
7. **alarm clock**
   будильник
8. **wardrobe**
   гардероб
9. **bed sheets**
   простыня
10. **nightstand**
    прикроватная тумба

Section B — Make a sentence

What is <u>on the left of</u> the <u>bed</u>?

There is a <u>lamp</u> on the left of the bed.

What are <u>on the right of</u> the <u>wardrobe</u>?

There are <u>drawers</u> on the right of the wardrobe.

Learn: on the left of, on the right of

Is there a <u>nightstand</u> <u>on the left of</u> the <u>bed</u>?

Yes, there is. / No, there isn't.

Are there <u>pillows</u> <u>on the left of</u> the <u>blanket</u>?

Yes, there are. / No, there aren't.

change – changing – changed – changed менять, меняться

My brother needs to **change** his bed sheets soon.

We will be **changing** our mattress for a harder one.

I **changed** my pillow last night and slept much better.

I haven't **changed** the light bulb in this lamp for two years.

Get up on the wrong side of the bed

Meaning: To describe somebody who is in a bad mood.

"Mom's in a really bad mood. I think she *got up on the wrong side of the bed*."

Trace and fill in the words

1. What is on the right of the bed?

There is a pillow on the right of the bed.

2. What is on the _____ of the nightstand?

_____ is a book on the left of the _____.

3. _____ is on the right of the _____?

_____ is a chair on the _____ of the wardrobe.

4. _____ _____ on the left of the bed?

There _____ a pillow on the left of the _____.

5. Is _____ a nightstand on the right of the bed?

No, there isn't.

6. _____ there blankets on the left of the mattress?

Yes, _____ are.

7. _____ there a _____ on the right of the drawers?

No, _____ _____.

8. Are there _____ on the left of the _____?

Yes, _____ _____.

In the bedroom!

Write the answers

alarm clock	bed	drawers

1. What is on the left of the bed?

_____.

2. Are the drawers on the right of the bed?

_____.

blanket	mattress	pillow

1. What is on the right of the mattress?

_____.

2. Is the pillow on the left of the mattress?

_____.

bed sheets	wardrobe	lamp

1. What is on the left of the wardrobe?

_____.

2. Is the lamp on the left of the wardrobe?

_____.

Write the answer next to the letter "A"

A: ___ **1.** ___ jeans are those? Those jeans are ___ .

a. Whose, hers   b. Who, her   c. Wear, on   d. Whose, her

A: ___ **2.** ___ those gloves his? Yes, ___ are.

a. Are, there   b. Are, they   c. Were, them   d. Do, they

A: ___ **3.** Can you ___ me your boots?

a. lent   b. lending   c. lend   d. has lent

A: ___ **4.** "The new shirt fits perfectly. It fits like a ___."

a. hat   b. sock   c. boot   d. glove

A: ___ **5.** Where ___ the books? ___ under the vase.

a. is, They   b. do, It's   c. are, They're   d. put, It's

A: ___ **6.** Is ___ a vase on the coffee table? No, there ___ .

a. it, wasn't   b. there, isn't   c. there, doesn't   d. he, isn't

A: ___ **7.** He hasn't ___ that new television yet.

a. move   b. moving   c. moves   d. moved

A: ___ **8.** "We don't have much time. We have to race against the ___."

a. clock   b. watch   c. car   d. team

A: ___ **9.** There ___ a bath mat ___ the bathtub.

a. are, above   b. have, on   c. be, in   d. is, beside

A: ___ **10.** Are ___ towels beside the mirror? No, there ___.

a. them, can't   b. there, aren't   c. have, hasn't   d. it, isn't

A: ___ **11.** He ___ the sink every Saturday afternoon.

a. wash   b. washing   c. washes   d. is wash

A: ___ **12.** "After failing many times, I decided to throw in the ___."

a. towel   b. quit   c. anger   d. ball

A: ___ **13.** There ___ drawers on the ___ of the wardrobe.

a. have, top   b. is, side   c. can, right   d. are, left

A: ___ **14.** Is ___ a lamp on the left of the bed? Yes, there ___.

a. it, have   b. there, is   c. they're, are   d. his, can

A: ___ **15.** We will ___ the blankets tomorrow.

a. changes   b. changing   c. change   d. changed

A: ___ **16.** "He's grumpy. I think he got up on the wrong side of the ___."

a. bed   b. lamp   c. happy   d. clock

Answers on page 206

Lesson 33: Around the house

возле дома

What will he be doing this weekend?
He will be fixing the gate.

Section A — Words

1. **work in the garage**
   работать в гараже
2. **fix the mailbox**
   починить почтовый ящик
3. **fix the gate**
   починить ворота
4. **work in the garden**
   работать в саду
5. **clean the pool**
   почистить бассейн

6. **work in the yard**
   работать во дворе
7. **fix the fence**
   починить забор
8. **clean the balcony**
   сделать уборку на балконе
9. **clean the outdoor furniture**
   почистить наружную мебель
10. **clean the barbecue**
    почистить гриль

Section B — Make a sentence

What will he be doing <u>this weekend</u>?

He will be <u>working in the garage</u>.

What won't she be doing <u>this weekend</u>?

She won't be <u>fixing the mailbox</u>.

Note: won't be = will not be, he'll = he will, she'll = she will

Will he be <u>working in the garden</u> <u>tomorrow</u>?

Yes, he will be. / No, he won't be.

Will you be <u>cleaning the barbecue</u> <u>tomorrow</u>?

Yes, I will be. / No, I won't be.

fix – fixing – fixed – fixed чинить

He **fixes** the fence every year.

My father is **fixing** the gate right now.

My uncle **fixed** our mailbox after the big storm last week.

I still haven't **fixed** the grammar mistakes in my report.

On the house

Meaning: To get something for free.

"The waiter apologized and gave him the meal *on the house*."

Trace and fill in the words

1. What will she be doing this weekend?

She will be working in the yard.

2. What will _____ be _____ this weekend?

He _____ be fixing the fence.

3. What _____ they be doing this _____?

_____ will be cleaning the balcony.

4. _____ will _____ be doing this _____?

He _____ _____ fixing the gate.

5. Will he be working in the garden tomorrow?

No, he won't _____.

6. Will we _____ cleaning the pool tomorrow?

Yes, _____ will _____.

7. _____ you be working in the garage _____?

Yes, _____ _____ _____.

8. Will they _____ cleaning the barbecue _____?

No, _____ _____ _____.

Around the house!

doing	weekend	this	
be	will	the	working

Write the words

What _____ she be doing this weekend?

She will _____ cleaning the balcony.

What will they be _____ this _____?

They will be fixing _____ fence.

What will you be doing _____ weekend?

I will be _____ in the yard.

don't, doesn't, didn't, won't, isn't, aren't, wasn't, weren't?

do not = __don't__   were not = _____

did not = _____   are not = _____

will not = _____   does not = _____

is not = _____   was not = _____

Lesson 34: Hobbies

хобби

What do you enjoy doing on the weekend?
I enjoy going hiking.

1. do gardening
заниматься садоводством
2. go hiking
ходить в поход
3. take photographs
снимать фотографии
4. play video games
играть в видеоигры
5. listen to music
слушать музыку

6. go camping
ездить в поход с ночлегом
7. play chess
играть в шахматы
8. watch movies
смотреть фильмы
9. go fishing
ездить на рыбалку
10. sing karaoke
петь караоке

What do you enjoy doing on the weekend?

I enjoy <u>doing gardening</u> on the weekend.

What does he enjoy doing on the weekend?

He enjoys <u>going camping</u> on the weekend.

Do you enjoy <u>going hiking</u> on the weekend?

Yes, I do. / No, I enjoy <u>playing chess</u>.

Does he enjoy <u>watching movies</u> on the weekend?

Yes, he does. / No, he enjoys <u>going fishing</u>.

enjoy – enjoying – enjoyed – enjoyed получать удовольствие

He **enjoys** doing the gardening in spring.

My aunt is **enjoying** the book you lent her.

I really **enjoyed** the movie we watched last night.

You would have **enjoyed** the video game we played today.

Face the music

Meaning: To face the consequences of one's actions.

"You need to own up to your mistake and *face the music*."

Trace and fill in the words

1. What do you enjoy doing on the weekend?

I enjoy going camping on the weekend.

2. What does _____ enjoy doing on the _____?

She _____ going hiking on the weekend.

3. _____ do they enjoy _____ on the weekend?

_____ enjoy singing karaoke on the _____.

4. What _____ he enjoy _____ on the _____?

_____ _____ playing chess on the _____.

5. Do you enjoy playing video games on the weekend?

No, I enjoy listening to music.

6. _____ he enjoy taking photographs on the weekend?

_____, _____ does.

7. _____ they _____ going hiking on the _____?

No, _____ enjoy _____ _____.

8. _____ she enjoy _____ chess on the _____?

Yes, _____ _____.

Hobbies!

Connect the words

listen •   • hiking

take •   • movies

go •   • chess

play •   • karaoke

watch •   • photographs

sing •   • to music

Enjoy or Enjoys?

1. He _____ listening to music on the weekend.

2. They _____ watching movies on the weekend.

3. We _____ going hiking on the weekend.

4. My brother _____ playing chess on the weekend.

5. She _____ taking photographs on the weekend.

6. I _____ playing video games on the weekend.

Answer the questions

1. What do you enjoy doing on the weekend?

_____.

2. What does your friend enjoy doing on the weekend?

_____.

Lesson 35: Countries

страны

Which countries have you been to?

I have been to Brazil and Mexico.

Section A — Words

1. Japan
Япония

2. Canada
Канада

3. Brazil
Бразилия

4. Australia
Австралия

5. South Africa
Южная Африка

6. China
Китай

7. Mexico
Мексика

8. Argentina
Аргентина

9. New Zealand
Новая Зеландия

10. Kenya
Кения

Section B — Make a sentence

Which countries have you been to?

I have been to <u>Japan</u> and <u>China</u>.

Which countries has she been to?

She has been to <u>Canada</u> and <u>Mexico</u>.

Note: haven't = have not / hasn't = has not

Have you been to <u>Brazil</u>?

Yes, I have. / No, I haven't.

Has he been to <u>Argentina</u>?

Yes, he has. / No, he hasn't.

write – writing – wrote – written писать

I always **write** homework on the weekend.

She is **writing** a new book about South Africa.

My father **wrote** a letter to his friend in Japan last week.

He has already **written** four emails to the factory in China.

Second to none

Meaning: To describe something that is the best.

"The mountains in Canada are *second to none* for skiing."

Trace and fill in the words

1. Which countries have you been to?

I have been to Canada and Mexico.

2. Which _____ has he been to?

He has _____ to Brazil and Argentina.

3. _____ countries _____ we been to?

We _____ been to _____ and _____.

4. Which _____ has she _____ _____?

_____ _____ been to _____ and _____.

5. Have you been to New Zealand?

Yes, I have.

6. Has _____ been _____ Australia?

_____, she hasn't.

7. _____ they _____ to China?

Yes, _____ _____.

8. _____ he _____ _____ Kenya?

No, _____ _____.

Countries!

Write the missing words

hasn't	they	has	been
to	countries	Which	haven't

1. Which _____ have you been to?

I have _____ to Japan and China.

2. _____ countries has he been to?

He _____ been to Mexico and Canada.

3. Has she been _____ South Africa?

No, she _____.

4. Have _____ been to New Zealand?

No, they _____.

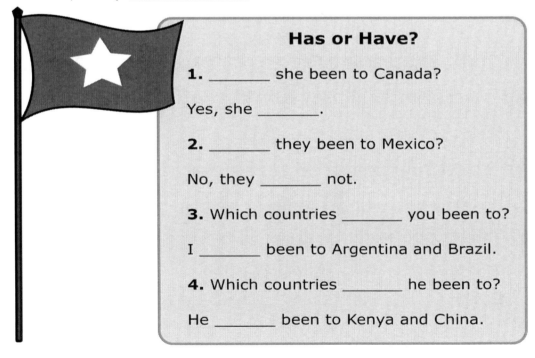

Has or Have?

1. _____ she been to Canada?

Yes, she _____.

2. _____ they been to Mexico?

No, they _____ not.

3. Which countries _____ you been to?

I _____ been to Argentina and Brazil.

4. Which countries _____ he been to?

He _____ been to Kenya and China.

Lesson 36: Landscapes

ландшафты

What had you prepared for yesterday's math class?

I had prepared a video about lakes.

Section A — Words

1. **river**
   река
2. **beach (es)**
   пляж
3. **mountain**
   гора
4. **volcano (es)**
   вулкан
5. **forest**
   лес

6. **lake**
   озеро
7. **waterfall**
   водопад
8. **island**
   остров
9. **ocean**
   океан
10. **jungle**
    джунгли

Section B — Make a sentence

What had you prepared for yesterday's <u>geography</u> class?

I had prepared a <u>poster</u> about <u>river</u>s.

What had they prepared for yesterday's <u>Chinese</u> class?

They had prepared an <u>article</u> about <u>lake</u>s.

Learn: poster, speech, video, article, presentation

Note: hadn't = had not

Section C Make a question

Had you prepared anything for yesterday's <u>English</u> class?

Yes, I had prepared a <u>speech</u>. / No, I hadn't.

Had you prepared anything for yesterday's <u>science</u> class?

Yes, I had prepared a <u>video</u>. / No, I hadn't.

Section D Learn a verb

prepare – preparing – prepared – prepared готовить

I'll **prepare** some food for you to take to the mountains.

She'll be **preparing** some drinks for the picnic at the lake.

The teacher always **prepared** a quiz for the students before.

I wish I had **prepared** more for the geography test.

Section E Learn an idiom

A drop in the ocean

Meaning: To only make a tiny impact.

"We donated money to the victims of the tsunami, but I'm afraid it is just *a drop in the ocean*."

Trace and fill in the words

1. What had you prepared for yesterday's geography class?

I had prepared an article about beaches.

2. What had he _____ for yesterday's _____ class?

He _____ prepared a speech _____ waterfalls.

3. What had they _____ for _____ _____ class?

They _____ _____ a video about mountains.

4. What had you _____ for _____ geography class?

_____ _____ _____ a poster about islands.

5. Had he prepared anything for yesterday's math class?

No, he hadn't.

6. Had you prepared _____ for yesterday's art class?

Yes, I _____ _____ a poster.

7. Had she _____ anything for _____ science class?

No, _____ _____ .

8. Had he prepared anything for yesterday's English class?

Yes, _____ had _____ a _____ .

Landscapes!

Unscramble the words and write

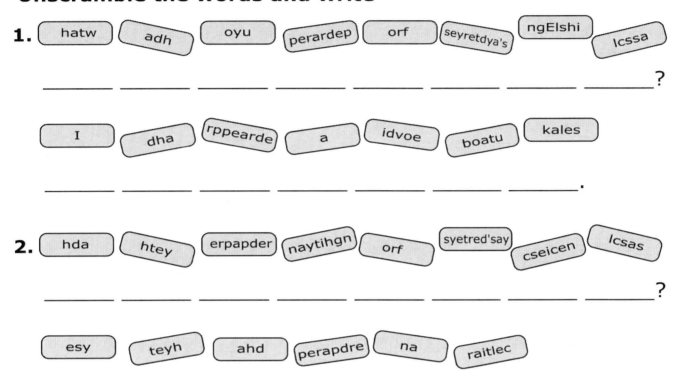

1. hatw · adh · oyu · perardep · orf · seyretdya's · ngElshi · lcssa

____ ____ ____ ____ ____ ____ ____ ____?

I · dha · rppearde · a · idvoe · boatu · kales

____ ____ ____ ____ ____ ____ ____.

2. hda · htey · erpapder · naytihgn · orf · syetred'say · cseicen · lcsas

____ ____ ____ ____ ____ ____ ____?

esy · teyh · ahd · perapdre · na · raitlec

____ , ____ ____ ____ ____ ____.

Complete the words

r__v__r   j__ng__e

v__l__a__o   i__la__d

m__un__a__n   f__r__ __t

be__c__   w__te__f__l__

o__e__n   l__k__

Write the answer next to the letter "A"

A: ___ **1.** ___ weekend, he will be ___ the mailbox.

a. On, clean   b. This, fixing   c. That, work   d. In, cleaning

A: ___ **2.** ___ she be fixing the gate tonight? Yes, she ___.

a. Can, is   b. Won't, fix   c. Will, will be   d. Will, fix

A: ___ **3.** My mother ___ the barbecue last year.

a. fix   b. is fixing   c. fixed   d. will fixing

A: ___ **4.** "This one's free. It's on the ___."

a. house   b. yard   c. gate   d. garage

A: ___ **5.** He ___ fishing on the weekend.

a. enjoy going   b. is enjoy go   c. enjoys go   d. enjoys going

A: ___ **6.** ___ he enjoy watching movies? No, he ___ playing chess.

a. Do, does   b. Is, isn't   c. Does, doesn't   d. Does, enjoys

A: ___ **7.** She is ___ her new barbecue.

a. enjoying   b. enjoy   c. enjoys   d. enjoyed

A: ___ **8.** "You should admit your mistake and face the ___."

a. sunshine   b. music   c. trouble   d. smile

A: ___ **9.** Which countries ___ you ___ to?

a. have, go   b. did, went   c. do, be   d. have, been

A: ___ **10.** ___ she been to Japan? No, she ___.

a. Has, hasn't   b. Have, don't   c. Is, hasn't   d. Is, can't

A: ___ **11.** He has ___ nine messages this week.

a. write   b. wrote   c. written   d. writes

A: ___ **12.** "Her English is the best. It's second to ___."

a. all   b. none   c. best   d. win

A: ___ **13.** They had ___ a speech for last week's geography class.

a. prepare   b. prepared   c. preparing   d. prepares

A: ___ **14.** ___ he prepared anything for English class? No, he ___.

a. Had, hadn't   b. Is, isn't   c. Does, don't   d. Has, haven't

A: ___ **15.** The teacher always ___ easy tests for his students.

a. prepare   b. preparing   c. prepares   d. are preparing

A: ___ **16.** "It had a very small effect. It was just a drop in the ___."

a. line   b. ball   c. water   d. ocean

Answers on page 206

Lesson 37: Everyday life

повседневная жизнь

When will you have woken up by?

I will have woken up by six o'clock.

1. **woken up**
   проснулся, проснулась
2. **brushed my teeth**
   почистил / почистила зубы
3. **done homework**
   сделал /сделала домашнее задание
4. **cooked dinner**
   приготовил / приготовила ужин
5. **taken out the trash**
   вынес мусор, вынесла мусор

6. **eaten breakfast**
   позавтракал, позавтракала
7. **gone to school**
   пошел / пошла в школу
8. **taken a shower**
   принял душ, принял душ
9. **gone to sleep**
   отправился / отправилась спать
10. **gone shopping**
    пошел / пошла за покупками

Section B Make a sentence

When will you have <u>woken up</u> by?

I will have woken up by <u>seven o'clock</u>.

When will he have <u>eaten breakfast</u> by?

He will have eaten breakfast by <u>half past eight</u>.

Learn: o'clock, half past, a quarter past, a quarter to

Will you have <u>taken a shower</u> by <u>nine o'clock</u>?

Yes, I will have. / No, I won't have.

Will they have <u>done homework</u> by <u>a quarter to six</u>?

Yes, they will have. / No, they won't have.

wake – waking – woke – woken будить

I **wake** up at seven o'clock every day.

The baby is **waking** up now.

You **woke** up late this morning.

I haven't **woken** up this early for years.

Hit the nail on the head

Meaning: To say something that is correct.

"I agree with what you said. You really *hit the nail on the head*."

Trace and fill in the words

1. When will you have woken up by?

I will have woken up by a quarter past seven.

2. When will he have _____ his teeth by?

He _____ have brushed his teeth by half past nine.

3. When _____ you _____ gone to school _____?

I will _____ gone to _____ by ten _____.

4. When will _____ have _____ homework by?

She will _____ done _____ by _____ o'clock.

5. Will they have cooked dinner by six o'clock?

No, they won't _____.

6. Will _____ have gone to sleep by _____ past ten?

Yes, we _____ _____.

7. _____ she _____ gone shopping by nine o'clock?

No, _____ _____ have.

8. _____ you have brushed _____ teeth by one o'clock?

Yes, _____ _____ _____.

Everyday life!

Unscramble the sentences

o'clock / gone / have / we / will / shopping / by / four

1. _____ .

two / taken / have / they / will / a shower / by / half past

2. _____ .

I / the trash / won't / one o'clock / have / by / taken out

3. _____ .

o'clock / cooked dinner / have / he / won't / by / six

4. _____ .

Connect the words

brushed•   • out the trash

gone •   • dinner

taken•   • my teeth

done•   • a shower

cooked•   • homework

taken•   • to sleep

Lesson 38: Languages

языки

How long have you been learning German?

I have been learning German for one year.

Section A — Words

1. **English**
   английский
2. **German**
   немецкий
3. **Portuguese**
   португальский
4. **Japanese**
   японский
5. **Vietnamese**
   вьетнамский

6. **Spanish**
   испанский
7. **French**
   французский
8. **Chinese**
   китайский
9. **Hindi**
   хинди
10. **Arabic**
    арабский

Section B — Make a sentence

How long have you been <u>learning English</u>?

I have been learning English for <u>three years</u>.

How long has he been <u>studying Spanish</u>?

He has been studying Spanish for <u>five months</u>.

Learn: learning, studying, speaking

Have they been <u>studying</u> <u>French</u> for a long time?

Yes, they have been. / No, they haven't been.

Has she been <u>learning</u> <u>Japanese</u> for a long time?

Yes, she has been. / No, she hasn't been.

speak – speaking – spoke – spoken говорить

He **speaks** three languages.

She is **speaking** to him in Japanese.

I **spoke** with my teacher about the German homework.

We haven't **spoken** to each other for over five years.

Speak the same language

Meaning: To share the same understanding and be in agreement.

"I agree with everything you are saying. I think we're *speaking the same language*."

Trace and fill in the words

1. How long have you been _____ German?

I have been learning German for three years.

2. How _____ has _____ been studying French?

She has _____ studying _____ for six years.

3. How _____ have we _____ learning _____?

_____ have been _____ English for three years.

4. _____ long have _____ been _____ Hindi?

They _____ been learning _____ for one year.

5. _____ they been speaking Arabic for a long time?

Yes, they have _____.

6. Has he been _____ Japanese for a long time?

No, _____ hasn't _____.

7. Have _____ been _____ Arabic for a long time?

Yes, I _____ _____.

8. Has she _____ studying _____ for a long time?

No, _____ _____ _____.

Languages!

| Mexico | France | Scotland | Japan | Egypt |

Write the Country, Question and Answer

| He | — | English | — | Three years | — | Scotland |

How long has he been learning English ?
He has been learning English for three years.

| They | — | Spanish | — | Ten years | — | |

_____ ?
_____ .

| She | — | Arabic | — | Four years | — | |

_____ ?
_____ .

| John | — | Japanese | — | One year | — | |

_____ ?
_____ .

| Susan | — | French | — | Two years | — | |

_____ ?
_____ .

How long have you been studying English?

_____ .

Lesson 39: Pets

домашние любимцы

What is faster than a mouse?

A rabbit is faster than a mouse.

Section A	Words

1. dog
собака

2. fish
рыба

3. bird
птица

4. rabbit
кролик

5. guinea pig
морская свинка

6. cat
кошка

7. turtle
черепаха

8. mouse
мышь

9. hamster
хомяк

10. snake
змея

Section B	Make a sentence

What is <u>bigger</u> than a <u>mouse</u>?

A <u>dog</u> is bigger than a mouse.

What is <u>more expensive</u> than the <u>hamster</u>?

The <u>rabbit</u> is more expensive than the hamster.

Learn: faster, slower, bigger, smaller, more expensive, cheaper, more colorful, better, worse

Is a <u>turtle</u> <u>slower</u> than a <u>guinea pig</u>?

Yes, it is. / No, it's not. It's <u>faster</u>.

Is the <u>bird</u> <u>more expensive</u> than the <u>snake</u>?

Yes, it is. / No, it's not. It's <u>cheaper</u>.

feed – feeding – fed – fed кормить

You need to **feed** the dog every morning.

He is **feeding** the turtle some leaves.

I **fed** the mouse some cheese and it happily ate it.

My sister hasn't **fed** the pets today.

The teacher's pet

Meaning: A student whom the teacher favors.

"Her classmates are jealous of her because she is *the teacher's pet.*"

Trace and fill in the words

1. What is bigger than a mouse?

A rabbit is _____ than a mouse.

2. What is more _____ _____ the dog?

The fish is _____ colorful than the _____.

3. _____ _____ slower than a _____?

A turtle is _____ _____ a cat.

4. What is less _____ _____ the snake?

_____ bird is _____ expensive than the _____.

5. Is the bird faster _____ the guinea pig?

Yes, _____ _____.

6. Is the rabbit more _____ than the dog?

No, _____ _____. It's cheaper.

7. _____ the turtle slower than the _____?

_____, _____ is.

8. Is the cat slower _____ the hamster?

No, it's _____. It's _____.

Pets!

Write the animals

	Animal	Speed	Size
	_____	48 km/h	30 cm
	_____	0.4 km/h	40 cm
	_____	13 km/h	9 cm
	_____	5 km/h	15 cm

Answer the questions

1. What is bigger than a fish? _____.

2. What is faster than a mouse? _____.

3. Is the turtle faster than the fish? _____.

4. Is the mouse slower than the rabbit? _____.

5. What is bigger than a rabbit? _____.

6. What is smaller than a fish? _____.

7. Is the rabbit bigger than the turtle? _____.

8. Is the rabbit bigger than the fish? _____.

Lesson 40: Fast food

фаст-фуд

What is the sweetest food?
The sweetest food is the pancake.

Section A — Words

1. **doughnut**
   бублик
2. **cheeseburger**
   чизбургер
3. **chicken nuggets**
   куриные наггеты
4. **pancake**
   блинчик
5. **taco**
   тако

6. **french fries**
   картофель-фри
7. **onion rings**
   колечки лука
8. **hot dog**
   хот-дог
9. **fried chicken**
   жареная курица
10. **burrito**
    буррито

Section B — Make a sentence

What is the <u>cheapest</u> food?

The cheapest food is the <u>doughnut</u>.

What is the <u>most expensive</u> food?

The most expensive food is the <u>burrito</u>.

Learn: most delicious, most expensive, cheapest, saltiest, sweetest, best, worst

Is the <u>hot dog</u> the <u>most delicious</u>?

Yes, it is. / No, it's not.

Are the <u>french fries</u> the <u>cheapest</u>?

Yes, they are. / No, they aren't.

try – trying – tried – tried пробовать

He wants to **try** the cheeseburger at that restaurant.

I'm **trying** to decide whether to buy the taco or burrito.

My baby brother **tried** the pancake, but didn't like it.

We haven't **tried** the fried chicken here yet.

You are what you eat

Meaning: The food that you eat affects your health.

"Careful not to eat too much fast food. *You are what you eat.*"

Trace and fill in the words

1. What is the cheapest food?

The _____ food is the taco.

2. What is the best _____?

The _____ food is the burrito.

3. _____ is the _____ delicious food?

_____ most _____ food is the doughnut.

4. _____ _____ the worst food?

_____ _____ food is _____ hot dog.

5. Is the most expensive food the cheeseburger?

No, it _____. It's the cheapest.

6. _____ the saltiest food _____ french fries?

Yes, _____ _____.

7. Is the most delicious _____ the fried chicken?

Yes, _____ _____.

8. Is _____ worst _____ _____ pancake?

No, it _____. It's _____ best.

Fast food!

Joe's Diner

doughnut	$2	french fries	$5
cheeseburger	$4	onion rings	$6
chicken nugget	$1	hot dog	$3
pancake	$6	fried chicken	$7
taco	$8	burrito	$9

Answer the questions

1. What is the most expensive food? _____.

2. What is the cheapest food? _____.

3. What is the saltiest food? _____.

4. What is the sweetest food? _____.

5. What is the most delicious food? _____.

6. Is the pancake the sweetest food? _____.

7. Is the taco the most delicious food? _____.

8. Are the french fries the saltiest food? _____.

Write the answer next to the letter "A"

A: ___ **1.** When ___ you have ___ to school by?

a. do, go   b. will, gone   c. can, went   d. will, go

A: ___ **2.** They will have ___ dinner by ___ six.

a. eat, o'clock b. ate, past   c. eats, quarter   d. eaten, half past

A: ___ **3.** They haven't ___ with each other for two years.

a. spoken   b. spokes   c. speaking   d. speaks

A: ___ **4.** "You said it exactly right. You hit the ___ on the head."

a. hammer   b. work   c. nail   d. day

A: ___ **5.** How long ___ he ___ learning Arabic?

a. does, is   b. is, can   c. have, does   d. has, been

A: ___ **6.** No, ___ haven't been ___ Spanish for a long time.

a. I, learn b. we, learned   c. they, learning   d. he, learns

A: ___ **7.** He ___ Chinese with the doctor last night.

a. spoke   b. is   c. was   d. speaks

A: ___ **8.** "I really agree with him. I think we ___ the same language."

a. speaks   b. speak   c. spoken   d. speaking

A: ___ **9.** What is ___ than a guinea pig?

a. cheaper   b. more cheap   c. more cheaper   d. cheapest

A: ___ **10.** Is the mouse ___ than the cat? No, it's ___.

a. slow, slower   b. big, smaller   c. slow, fast   d. slower, faster

A: ___ **11.** We haven't ___ the pets yet.

a. feed   b. fed   c. feeding   d. feeds

A: ___ **12.** "The teacher really loved him. He was the teacher's ___."

a. pets   b. petting   c. pet   d. best

A: ___ **13.** What is the ___ food on the menu?

a. more cheap   b. cheapest   c. most cheap   d. cheapen

A: ___ **14.** ___ the taco the ___ delicious?

a. Had, more   b. Is, more   c. Does, most   d. Is, most

A: ___ **15.** He usually ___ new food every weekend.

a. try   b. trying   c. tries   d. had try

A: ___ **16.** "You should eat healthier food. You ___ what you eat."

a. are   b. can   c. do   d. try

Answers on page 206

Lesson 41: At the cinema

в кинотеатре

> What was the romance movie like?
>
> It was romantic.

Section A | **Words**

1. **scary**
   страшный
2. **exciting**
   интересный, захватывающий
3. **informative**
   познавательный
4. **romantic**
   романтический
5. **violent**
   агрессивный, с насилием

6. **boring**
   скучный
7. **interesting**
   интересный
8. **funny**
   смешной
9. **enjoyable**
   приятный
10. **sad**
    печальный, грустный

Section B | **Make a sentence**

What was the <u>horror</u> movie like?

It was <u>scary</u>.

What was the <u>action</u> movie like?

It was <u>exciting</u>.

Learn: horror, comedy, action, romance, sci-fi, animation

Was the <u>horror</u> movie as <u>exciting</u> as the <u>action</u> movie?

Yes, it was. / No, it wasn't.

Was the <u>sci-fi</u> movie as <u>funny</u> as the <u>comedy</u> movie?

Yes, it was. / No, it wasn't.

teach – teaching – taught – taught учить

The movie **teaches** us about looking after the environment.

My father will be **teaching** me how to swim.

My history teacher **taught** us interesting things this year.

The teacher hasn't **taught** us anything informative yet.

A tough act to follow

Meaning: Someone who did so well that it would be hard to do better.

"He was so funny in this movie. It will be *a tough act to follow*."

Trace and fill in the words

1. What was the comedy movie like?

It was really funny.

2. What _____ the romance movie _____?

_____ was romantic.

3. _____ _____ the sci-fi movie like?

_____ _____ really exciting.

4. What _____ _____ animation movie _____?

_____ _____ enjoyable.

5. Was the _____ movie as funny as the comedy movie?

No, it _____.

6. Was the action movie as _____ as the horror movie?

Yes, _____ _____.

7. _____ the animation movie as sad as the sci-fi movie?

_____, _____ wasn't.

8. Was the horror _____ as violent as the action movie?

_____, it _____.

At the cinema!

True of False? Circle the answer

1. The comedy movie was funny.   **True**   **False**

2. The romance movie was informative.   **True**   **False**

3. The action movie was exciting.   **True**   **False**

4. The sci-fi movie was sad.   **True**   **False**

Complete the words

b__r__ng   i__fo__ma__i__e   e__jo__ab__e

i__t__r__s__in__   e__c__tin__   sc__r__

f__n__y   r__m__nt__c   v__o__en__

Lesson 42: Music

музыка

How does she play the violin?
She plays the violin gracefully.

Section A — Words

1. **beautifully**
   красиво
2. **quietly**
   тихо
3. **slowly**
   медленно
4. **gracefully**
   элегантно, грациозно
5. **well**
   хорошо

6. **loudly**
   громко
7. **quickly**
   быстро
8. **terribly**
   ужасно
9. **correctly**
   правильно
10. **badly**
    плохо

Section B — Make a sentence

How does he <u>sing the song</u>?

He sings the song <u>beautifully</u>.

How do they <u>play the guitar</u>?

They play the guitar <u>loudly</u>.

Learn: sing the song, play the piano, play the violin, play the cello, play the drums, play the guitar

Does she <u>play the violin</u> <u>gracefully</u>?

Yes, she does. / No, she doesn't.

Do you <u>play the drums</u> <u>well</u>?

Yes, I do. / No, I don't.

notice – noticing – noticed – noticed замечать

You will **notice** that my family speaks loudly.

I'm **noticing** more and more how well she speaks English.

I **noticed** you haven't done your homework correctly.

She hadn't **noticed** her friend looking at her.

Music to one's ears

Meaning: Something very pleasing to hear.

"It was *music to my ears* when I heard that the teacher cancelled the test!"

Trace and fill in the words

1. How does _____ play the piano?

She plays the _____ quickly.

2. _____ do we play the _____?

_____ play the violin terribly.

3. How _____ he play _____ cello?

He _____ the cello gracefully.

4. _____ _____ you play the drums?

_____ _____ the drums well.

5. Does he play the trumpet correctly?

Yes, _____ does.

6. _____ you sing the song beautifully?

No, _____ don't.

7. _____ she _____ the cello correctly?

Yes, _____ does.

8. _____ _____ play _____ guitar quietly?

No, they _____.

Music!

Write the correct verb

1. **play/plays?** He _____ the piano beautifully.

2. **sing/sings?** She _____ the song quietly.

3. **play/plays?** They _____ the violin badly.

4. **play/plays?** We _____ the guitar well.

Write the sentences

1. plays the piano - quick

   _She plays the piano quickly_____.

2. sings the song - beautiful

   _____.

3. plays the trumpet - loud

   _____.

4. plays the cello - bad

   _____.

Lesson 43: Feelings

чувства

How have you been feeling lately?

Lately, I've been feeling tired.

Section A   Words

1. **sad**
   печальный
2. **tired**
   усталый
3. **fine**
   хороший, замечательный
4. **bored**
   скучающий
5. **energetic**
   энергичный

6. **happy**
   счастливый
7. **sick**
   больной
8. **angry**
   сердитый
9. **excited**
   радостный, возбужденный
10. **frustrated**
    расстроенный, раздосадованный

Section B   Make a sentence

How have you been feeling lately?

Lately, I've been feeling <u>sad</u>.

How are you now?

I'm <u>happy</u>.

Note: I've = I have / she's = she has / he's = he has
they've = they have / we've = we have / you've = you have

Have you been feeling <u>tired</u> lately?

Yes, I have. / No, I haven't.

Are you <u>angry</u>?

Yes, I am. / No, I'm not.

think – thinking – thought – thought думать

I **think** she feels fine now. Thank you for your concern.

She's frustrated because she keeps **thinking** about work.

Peter **thought** about how excited his child was to see him.

I haven't **thought** about this before.

Mixed Feelings

Meaning: When you are not sure about how you feel about something.

"He had *mixed feelings* about moving to a new city."

Trace and fill in the words

1. How have you been feeling lately?

Lately, I've been feeling tired.

2. How has she _____ feeling lately?

Lately, she's been _____ angry.

3. How _____ they been _____ lately?

Lately, they've _____ feeling bored.

4. How _____ he _____ feeling _____?

Lately, _____ been _____ _____.

5. Have you been feeling excited lately?

No, I haven't.

6. Has he been _____ energetic lately?

Yes, _____ _____.

7. Have _____ _____ feeling frustrated lately?

Yes, I _____.

8. _____ he been _____ sick _____?

No, _____ _____.

Feelings!

Match the face with the word

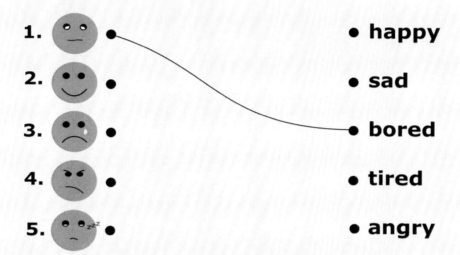

1. • ——————— • happy

2. • • sad

3. • • bored

4. • • tired

5. • • angry

Answer the questions

1. How has he been feeling lately?
<u>Lately, he's been feeling bored</u> .

2. How has she been feeling lately?
_____.

3. How have they been feeling lately?
_____.

4. Has she been feeling tired lately?
_____.

5. Has he been feeling angry lately?
_____.

How have you been feeling lately?

_____.

Lesson 44: The calendar

календарь

When is your competition?
My competition is on the 2nd of May.

1. **birthday**
   день рождения
2. **competition**
   соревнование
3. **class**
   занятие, урок
4. **speech**
   речь, выступление
5. **party**
   вечеринка

6. **meeting**
   встреча
7. **appointment**
   назначенная встреча, визит
8. **test**
   экзамен
9. **day off**
   выходной
10. **recital**
    концерт, выступление

When is your <u>birthday</u>?

My birthday is on the <u>21st</u> of <u>February</u>.

Learn: January, February, March, April, May, June, July, August, September, October, November, December

1st 2nd 3rd 4th 5th 6th 7th 8th 9th 10th 11th 12th 13th 14th 15th 16th 17th 18th 19th 20th 21st 22nd 23rd 24th 25th 26th 27th 28th 29th 30th 31st

Is your <u>meeting</u> on the <u>12th</u> of <u>November</u>?

Yes, it is. / No, it isn't.

Was your <u>party</u> on the <u>10th</u> of <u>June</u>?

Yes, it was. / No, it wasn't.

organize – organizing – organized – organized организовывать

She will **organize** a meeting for this Friday.

Fran is **organizing** a person to help me with the recital.

The teacher **organized** a speech competition at school.

She has **organized** many parties for the company.

Make a date

Meaning: To arrange a meeting with someone.

"We should *make a date* and discuss this further."

Trace and fill in the words

1. When is your appointment?

My appointment is on the 22nd of September.

2. When _____ his competition?

His _____ is on the 31st of October.

3. When is their test?

_____ _____ is on the 11th of _____.

4. When _____ _____ party?

Her _____ is _____ _____ 12th of _____.

5. Is your recital on the 15th of November?

No, _____ isn't.

6. Was his speech _____ the 18th of _____?

No, it _____.

7. Is her day off _____ the _____ of _____?

Yes, _____ _____.

8. Was their class _____ the _____ _____ May?

_____, it _____.

The calendar!

May						
Monday	**Tuesday**	**Wednesday**	**Thursday**	**Friday**	**Saturday**	**Sunday**
	1st	2nd	3rd	4th Meeting	5th	6th
7th	8th Recital	9th	10th	11th	12th	13th
14th	15th	16th	17th Birthday	18th	19th	20th
21st	22nd Test	23rd	24th	25th	26th Party	27th
28th Day off	29th	30th	31st			

Answer the questions

1. When is your birthday?

_____.

2. When is your test?

_____.

3. Is your party on the 26th of May?

_____.

4. Was your test on the 22nd of April?

_____.

Write the answer next to the letter "A"

A: ___ **1.** ___ was the horror movie ___? It was scary.

a. How, like   b. When, see   c. Where, like   d. What, like

A: ___ **2.** Was the comedy as funny ___ the action movie?

a. movie   b. watch   c. like   d. as

A: ___ **3.** His mother ___ how to swim.

a. teach him   b. taught him   c. teaches he   d. learn him

A: ___ **4.** "Her speech was great. It will be a tough ___ to follow."

a. day   b. act   c. song   d. beat

A: ___ **5.** She ___ the piano ___ every Saturday night.

a. plays, well   b. play, quickly   c. playing, slowly   d. play, bad

A: ___ **6.** Does he ___ the drums ___ for this song?

a. play, correctly   b. play, good   c. plays, well   d. plays, badly

A: ___ **7.** He hadn't ___ his friend speaking Chinese to him.

a. notice   b. notices   c. noticed   d. noticing

A: ___ **8.** "It's such good news! It's ___ to my ears."

a. singing   b. dancing   c. sound   d. music

A: ___ **9.** Lately, she ___ been ___ happy.

a. have, feeling   b. is, felt   c. has, feeling   d. does, feels

A: ___ **10.** ___ you been feeling ___ lately? No, I haven't been.

a. Do, tired   b. Can, tired   c. Have, tired   d. Have, tire

A: ___ **11.** Todd wasn't ___ excited during gym class yesterday.

a. feeling   b. feel   c. feels   d. felt

A: ___ **12.** "He wasn't sure what to do. He had ___ feelings."

a. mixing   b. mixed   c. mix   d. mixes

A: ___ **13.** When is ___ birthday? His birthday is on ___ 10th of May.

a. him, it   b. he's, a   c. he's, one   d. his, the

A: ___ **14.** Is ___ recital on the 15th of November? No, it ___.

a. her, isn't   b. his, doesn't   c. your, can't   d. my, won't

A: ___ **15.** Fran is ___ a group of people to help us.

a. organize   b. organizing   c. organizes   d. organized

A: ___ **16.** "Let's arrange a meeting. We should make a ___."

a. meet   b. test   c. date   d. try

Answers on page 206

Test 1
1. a   2. c   3. a   4. d   5. d   6. c   7. c   8. b   9. d   10. b   11. b   12. a   13. a   14. a
15. c   16. d

Test 2
1. b   2. c   3. c   4. d   5. a   6. b   7. d   8. b   9. d   10. a   11. c   12. c   13. d   14. c
15. b   16. d

Test 3
1. d   2. b   3. d   4. c   5. b   6. a   7. c   8. a   9. d   10. c   11. c   12. d   13. a   14. c
15. c   16. d

Test 4
1. d   2. b   3. c   4. c   5. d   6. d   7. a   8. d   9. b   10. b   11. c   12. b   13. d   14. d
15. a   16. d

Test 5
1. a   2. a   3. c   4. b   5. d   6. d   7. b   8. a   9. c   10. d   11. c   12. b   13. d   14. c
15. a   16. c

Test 6
1. b   2. b   3. a   4. d   5. c   6. c   7. d   8. b   9. a   10. d   11. a   12. b   13. b   14. c
15. c   16. c

Test 7
1. c   2. c   3. b   4. a   5. b   6. a   7. c   8. d   9. d   10. c   11. a   12. c   13. b   14. b
15. d   16. d

Test 8
1. a   2. b   3. c   4. d   5. c   6. b   7. d   8. a   9. d   10. b   11. c   12. a   13. d   14. b
15. c   16. a

Test 9
1. b   2. c   3. c   4. a   5. d   6. d   7. a   8. b   9. d   10. a   11. c   12. b   13. b   14. a
15. c   16. d

Test 10
1. b   2. d   3. a   4. c   5. d   6. c   7. a   8. b   9. a   10. d   11. b   12. c   13. b   14. d
15. c   16. a

Test 11
1. d   2. d   3. b   4. b   5. a   6. a   7. c   8. d   9. c   10. c   11. a   12. b   13. d   14. a
15. b   16. c

Preston Lee's

Conversation
ENGLISH

Lesson 1 - 40

For Russian Speakers

CONTENTS

Lesson 1: My family моя семья — Page 212

Lesson 2: My pencil case мой пенал — Page 216

Lesson 3: In the classroom в классе — Page 220

Lesson 4: The weather погода — Page 224

Lesson 5: Places места — Page 228

Lesson 6: Sports спорт — Page 232

Lesson 7: At the zoo в зоопарке — Page 236

Lesson 8: Colors цвета — Page 240

Lesson 9: Activities занятия — Page 244

Lesson 10: Food & Drinks еда и напитки — Page 248

Lesson 11: At the fruit market на фруктовом рынке — Page 252

Lesson 12: Shapes фигуры — Page 256

Lesson 13: At the supermarket в супермаркете — Page 260

Lesson 14: At the ice cream shop в магазине мороженого — Page 264

Lesson 15: In the refrigerator в холодильнике — Page 268

Lesson 16: Jobs работа — Page 272

Lesson 17: Names имена — Page 276

Lesson 18: More places еще места — Page 280

Lesson 19: Meats мясо — Page 284

Lesson 20: Vegetables овощи — Page 288

Lesson 21: At school в школе   Page 292

Lesson 22: School subjects школьные предметы   Page 296

Lesson 23: Chores работа по дому   Page 300

Lesson 24: At the toy store в магазине игрушек   Page 304

Lesson 25: In the kitchen в кухне   Page 308

Lesson 26: In the toolbox в ящике для инструментов   Page 312

Lesson 27: Transportation транспорт   Page 316

Lesson 28: Clothes одежда   Page 320

Lesson 29: More clothes ещё одежда   Page 324

Lesson 30: In the living room в гостиной   Page 328

Lesson 31: In the bathroom в ванной комнате   Page 332

Lesson 32: In the bedroom в спальне   Page 336

Lesson 33: Around the house возле дома   Page 340

Lesson 34: Hobbies хобби   Page 344

Lesson 35: Countries страны   Page 348

Lesson 36: Landscapes ландшафты   Page 352

Lesson 37: Everyday life повседневная жизнь   Page 356

Lesson 38: Languages языки   Page 360

Lesson 39: Pets домашние любимцы   Page 364

Lesson 40: Fast food фаст-фуд   Page 368

Answers   Page 372

Lesson 1: My family

моя семья

Who is she?
She is my baby sister.

Learn the words

1. **mother**
   мать
2. **grandmother**
   бабушка
3. **sister**
   сестра
4. **baby sister**
   сестренка
5. **aunt**
   тётя

6. **father**
   отец
7. **grandfather**
   дедушка
8. **brother**
   брат
9. **baby brother**
   братишка
10. **uncle**
    дядя

Learn a verb

see – seeing – saw – seen видеть

Peter: I haven't seen your brother for a long time. How is he?

Learn an idiom

Like one of the family

Meaning: To be like a person in one's family.

"Our dog is treated *like one of the family*."

Peter: Hey, Mary. What are you doing this weekend?

Mary: I'm going to my aunt's birthday party.

Peter: Great! Will many people be there?

Mary: No, just the family will be there.

Peter: I thought your grandfather was in hospital?

Mary: That's right. My grandfather won't be going to the party.

Peter: How is your grandfather feeling now?

Mary: My grandmother said he's feeling better.

Peter: Did you get your aunt a gift?

Mary: No. My brother and I are still deciding what to get her.

Peter: I haven't seen your brother for a long time. How is he?

Mary: He's fine. He's playing tennis with my sister now.

Peter: I didn't know he plays tennis.

Mary: He has been learning for six months.

Peter: My mother plays tennis really well.

Mary: I saw her at the park. She was with your baby sister.

Peter: They were walking the dog.

Mary: Your dog is so cute. It really loves your baby sister.

Peter: I know. It's like one of the family.

Mary: Hey, Peter. Is he your father?

Peter: No, he isn't.

Mary: Who is he?

Peter: He is my uncle. I better go. Have fun at the party!

Fill in the blanks

Peter: Hey, Mary. What _____ you doing this _____?

Mary: I'm _____ to my aunt's _____ party.

Peter: How is _____ grandfather _____ now?

Mary: My grandmother _____ he's feeling _____.

Peter: I haven't seen your brother for a long _____. How is he?

Mary: He's fine. He's _____ tennis with my sister _____.

Peter: I _____ know he _____ tennis.

Answer the questions

1. What is Mary doing this weekend?

_____

2. Where is Mary's grandfather?

_____

3. What is Mary's brother doing now?

_____

4. How long has Mary's brother been playing tennis?

_____

5. Who did Mary see at the park?

_____

Write the answer next to the letter "A"

A: ___ **1.** Mary's ___ is having a birthday party this weekend.

a. uncle   b. mother   c. aunt   d. sister

A: ___ **2.** Mary's ___ won't be going to the party.

a. grandfather   b. father   c. brother   d. uncle

A: ___ **3.** Does Mary have a gift for her aunt?

a. Yes, she does.   b. No, she doesn't.   c. Yes, she is.   d. No, she isn't.

A: ___ **4.** Mary's brother is playing ___ with her ___.

a. soccer, sister   b. tennis, sister   c. golf, aunt   d. tennis, mother

A: ___ **5.** How long has Mary's brother been learning tennis?

a. Six days.   b. Six weeks.   c. Seven months.   d. Six months.

A: ___ **6.** Peter's dog is like one of the ___.

a. animals   b. family   c. people   d. friends

A: ___ **7.** The dog really loves Peter's ___.

a. mother   b. father   c. baby sister   d. aunt

A: ___ **8.** Who did Mary see?

a. Peter's father.   b. Peter's uncle.   c. Peter's brother.   d. Peter's aunt.

Answers on page 372

Lesson 2: My pencil case

мой пенал

What is this?

It is an eraser.

Learn the words

1. a pencil
карандаш

2. an eraser
ластик

3. glue
клей

4. a pencil sharpener
точилка

5. whiteout
корректор

6. a pen
ручка

7. a ruler
линейка

8. tape
липкая лента

9. a marker
маркер

10. a crayon
мелок

Learn a verb

buy – buying – bought – bought покупать

Kevin: Sorry. Here's my ruler. I bought it yesterday.

Learn an idiom

Cross your fingers

Meaning: To wish for luck.

"*Cross your fingers* and hope this marker has ink."

Jessica: Hi, Kevin. I forgot my pencil case.

Kevin: We have art class now. You will need it.

Jessica: I know. Can I borrow your pencils?

Kevin: I'm using crayons to draw my picture. I didn't bring pencils.

Jessica: Okay. I want to draw a house, so I'll need a ruler.

Kevin: That's fine. You can use mine. Here you go.

Jessica: What is this?

Kevin: It's a ruler.

Jessica: No, it isn't. It's an eraser.

Kevin: Sorry. Here's my ruler.

Jessica: What are you going to draw?

Kevin: I don't know what I should draw.

Jessica: The teacher wants us to draw our home.

Kevin: I think I'm going to draw the classroom.

Jessica: Is the classroom your home?

Kevin: No, but it feels like it. We are here all day, every day!

Jessica: I'm not sure if the teacher will like that.

Kevin: She'll think it's funny.

Jessica: Cross your fingers she won't be angry!

Kevin: I want to stick pictures on my paper. Look at these pictures.

Jessica: They look good. Do you have any tape?

Kevin: No, I don't, but I bought some glue last Friday.

Jessica: Hey, Kevin. That's whiteout, not glue!

Unscramble the sentences

1. to / picture / my / I'm / draw / crayons / using

_____

2. our / wants / teacher / to / draw / The / home / us

_____

3. stick / on / to / I / paper / want / my / pictures

_____

Answer the questions

1. What class are they in?

_____

2. What did Jessica forget to bring?

_____

3. Why does Jessica want to use a ruler?

_____

4. What does Kevin want to draw?

_____

5. Does Kevin have any tape?

_____

Write the answer next to the letter "A"

A: ___ **1.** Jessica ___ her pencil case.

a. forgets   b. forgot   c. forget   d. forgotten

A: ___ **2.** Kevin and Jessica are in ___ class now.

a. math   b. art   c. science   d. English

A: ___ **3.** Will Kevin draw a house?

a. Yes, he will.   b. No, he doesn't.   c. Yes, he does.   d. No, he won't.

A: ___ **4.** Jessica wanted to borrow a ___ from Kevin.

a. eraser   b. ruler   c. whiteout   d. marker

A: ___ **5.** Kevin wants to use ___ to draw his picture.

a. markers   b. pencils   c. pens   d. crayons

A: ___ **6.** The teacher wants the students to draw their ___.

a. apartment   b. house   c. home   d. classroom

A: ___ **7.** Kevin ___ some ___ last Friday.

a. bought, glue   b. bought, tape   c. buys, glue   d. buys, tape

A: ___ **8.** Kevin will use ___ to stick the pictures on the paper.

a. eraser   b. whiteout   c. tape   d. glue

Answers on page 372

Lesson 3: In the Classroom

в классе

What are these?

These are old books.

Learn the words

1. **chair**
   стул
2. **blackboard**
   доска для мела
3. **poster**
   плакат
4. **globe**
   глобус
5. **clock**
   часы

6. **desk**
   парта
7. **whiteboard**
   доска для маркера
8. **bookshelf**
   книжная полка
9. **computer**
   компьютер
10. **book**
    книга

Learn a verb

look – looking – looked – looked смотреть, выглядеть

Susan: I was looking at your classroom before. It looks great.

Learn an idiom

Class clown

Meaning: A student who often makes everyone laugh in the classroom.

"Peter is the *class clown*. Even the teacher laughs sometimes."

Matthew: Hi, Susan. Did you have fun on your holidays?

Susan: Yes, I did. I traveled to Canada for two weeks.

Matthew: That sounds excellent! How was it?

Susan: It was so much fun! I learned how to ski.

Matthew: My holidays were boring. I'm happy school has started.

Susan: I'm not happy to be back at school!

Matthew: Why? I thought you loved school.

Susan: I like school, but I'm angry about my new classroom.

Matthew: Really? Why?

Susan: It has a really old computer and there's no whiteboard.

Matthew: That's too bad. My classroom has new desks and chairs.

Susan: I was looking at your classroom before. It looks great.

Matthew: I'm lucky this year. Last year, the clock was broken.

Susan: Your bookshelf also has many new books.

Matthew: Doesn't your classroom have new books?

Susan: No, they're all old, but we do have a new globe.

Matthew: What happened to the other globe?

Susan: The teacher said John knocked it off her desk.

Matthew: The teacher must have been really angry at him!

Susan: He didn't mean to push it. He was dancing like a robot.

Matthew: John really is the class clown.

Susan: That's true. He can be so funny sometimes.

Matthew: We better go to class. We'll talk at lunch.

Find the mistakes and write the sentence correctly

Susan: It has a really new computer and there's no blackboard.

_____

Matthew: I'm lucky this week. Last year, the globe was broken.

_____

Susan: No, they're all new, but we do have an old bookshelf.

_____

Answer the questions

1. How long was Susan in Canada for?

_____

2. What did Susan learn how to do?

_____

3. Is Susan happy to be back at school?

_____

4. What was broken in Matthew's classroom last year?

_____

5. What was John dancing like?

_____

Write the answer next to the letter "A"

A: ___ **1.** Susan ___ to ___ for two weeks.

a. travel, Canada   b. traveled, Canada   c. will travel, USA   d. travel, USA

A: ___ **2.** Matthew thinks his holidays ___ boring.

a. are   b. is   c. were   d. was

A: ___ **3.** Susan ___ angry about her new classroom.

a. feels   b. feel   c. feeling   d. fell

A: ___ **4.** Susan's new classroom doesn't have a ___.

a. computer   b. poster   c. blackboard   d. whiteboard

A: ___ **5.** "I ___ looking at your classroom. It ___ great."

a. were, looking   b. am, looks   c. was, look   d. was, looks

A: ___ **6.** When was the clock in Matthew's classroom broken?

a. Two years ago.   b. Last year.   c. This year.   d. Last month.

A: ___ **7.** Susan's ___ classroom has ___ books.

a. new, old   b. old, new   c. big, old   d. old, big

A: ___ **8.** The teacher ___ John knocked it ___ her desk.

a. says, off   b. said, of   c. say, of   d. said, off

Answers on page 372

Lesson 4: The weather

погода

How is the weather on Friday?

It is sunny.

Learn the words

1. **snowy**
   снег
2. **sunny**
   солнечно
3. **rainy**
   дождливо
4. **windy**
   ветрено
5. **cloudy**
   облачно

6. **hot**
   жарко
7. **cold**
   холодно
8. **warm**
   тепло
9. **cool**
   прохладно
10. **freezing**
    морозно

Learn a verb

feel – feeling – felt – felt чувствовать

Tom: It's surrounded by trees. We won't feel the wind there.

Learn an idiom

It's raining cats and dogs

Meaning: It's raining heavily.

"You can't play outside right now. *It's raining cats and dogs.*"

Tom: Do you want to play basketball with me on Saturday?

John: Sure. Where do you want to play?

Tom: We can play at the park.

John: Which park?

Tom: The big park that is next to the swimming pool.

John: If we want to play outside, we better check the weather.

Tom: How is the weather on Saturday?

John: It is cold and rainy.

Tom: Are you sure? It's been sunny all week.

John: Yes, I think it's going to rain cats and dogs.

Tom: How about on Sunday? Will it be warm enough to play?

John: Let me check.

Tom: I'm okay with cold weather as long as it's not freezing.

John: The weather is cloudy on Sunday, but no rain.

Tom: Sounds good. Let's play basketball on Sunday.

John: It might be windy at the park.

Tom: It's fine. We'll play on basketball court 2.

John: Why that one?

Tom: It's surrounded by trees. We won't feel the wind there.

John: Great! What time do you want to meet?

Tom: Let's get there early when nobody is playing.

John: I can arrive at eight o'clock.

Tom: Perfect! I'll see you at the big park at eight.

Put the sentences in order

John: Which park? ____

Tom: We can play at the park. ____

Tom: How is the weather on Saturday? ____

John: Sure. Where do you want to play? ____

Tom: Do you want to play basketball with me on Saturday? ____

John: If we want to play outside, we better check the weather. ____

John: It is cold and rainy. ____

Tom: The big park that is next to the swimming pool. ____

Answer the questions

1. Which sport does Tom want to play?

_____

2. How is the weather on Saturday?

_____

3. Which park does Tom want to play basketball at?

_____

4. Why does Tom want to play on basketball court 2?

_____

5. What time will they meet at the park?

_____

Write the answer next to the letter "A"

A: ___ **1.** What ___ the boys want to play? They ___ to play basketball.

a. does, wants   b. do, want   c. will, want   d. will, wants

A: ___ **2.** They will play basketball at the big park next to the ___.

a. swimming pool   b. school   c. park   d. home

A: ___ **3.** Will they play basketball on Saturday?

a. Yes, they will.   b. No, they won't.   c. Yes, they did.   d. No, they don't.

A: ___ **4.** The weather is ___ on Saturday.

a. sunny and hot   b. cold and windy   c. sunny and warm   d. cold and rainy

A: ___ **5.** The weather is ___ on Sunday, but no ___.

a. windy, rain   b. cold, rain   c. cloudy, rain   d. freezing, snow

A: ___ **6.** They will play on basketball court 2 because of the ___.

a. cold   b. rain   c. wind   d. sun

A: ___ **7.** Basketball court 2 is surrounded by ___.

a. walls   b. a fence   c. a tree   d. trees

A: ___ **8.** The boys will meet at ___ on ___.

a. Saturday, eight   b. eight, Saturday   c. Sunday, eight   d. eight, Sunday

Answers on page 372

Lesson 5: Places

места

Where is he going?

He is going to the gym.

Learn the words

1. **park**
   парк
2. **beach**
   пляж
3. **night market**
   ночной рынок
4. **store**
   магазин
5. **supermarket**
   супермаркет

6. **restaurant**
   ресторан
7. **swimming pool**
   бассейн
8. **department store**
   универмаг
9. **cinema**
   кинотеатр
10. **gym**
    спортзал

Learn a verb

walk – walking – walked – walked ходить

Peter: We first walked around the supermarket. That was boring.

Learn an idiom

Have a change of heart

Meaning: To change your mind about something.

"I've *had a change of heart* about this place. Let's go to another restaurant."

Peter: Hi, Kevin. What did you do last weekend?

Kevin: I went swimming.

Peter: Where did you go swimming?

Kevin: At first, Dad wanted to go to the beach, but it was too cold.

Peter: I agree. The water would have been freezing at the beach!

Kevin: Dad decided to take me to the swimming pool instead.

Peter: Do you mean the swimming pool next to the big park?

Kevin: Yes, that's right.

Peter: Mary is going to that swimming pool now.

Kevin: I like that one because it has warm water.

Peter: Last week, you said you were going to see a movie, right?

Kevin: I had a change of heart about going to the cinema.

Peter: Really? Why?

Kevin: Because I haven't been exercising much lately.

Peter: That's true. I haven't seen you at the gym for a long time.

Kevin: How about you? What did you do on the weekend?

Peter: I went shopping with Mom.

Kevin: Was that fun?

Peter: Yes and no.

Kevin: What do you mean?

Peter: We first walked around the supermarket. That was boring.

Kevin: And then?

Peter: Later, we went to the night market. That was a lot of fun.

Fill in the blanks

Kevin: Dad _____ to take me to the swimming pool _____.

Peter: Do you mean the _____ pool next to the big _____?

Kevin: I had a _____ of heart about going to the _____.

Peter: Mary is _____ to that swimming pool _____.

Kevin: How _____ you? What did you do on the _____?

Peter: I _____ shopping with _____.

Peter: We first walked around the _____. That was _____.

Answer the questions

1. What did Kevin do last weekend?

_____

2. Where did Kevin's father first want to go?

_____

3. Why did Kevin have a change of heart about seeing a movie?

_____

4. Where is Mary going now?

_____

5. What did Peter think about walking around the supermarket?

_____

Write the answer next to the letter "A"

A: ___ **1.** Kevin and his father ___ to the beach because it was too cold.

a. don't go   b. didn't go   c. doesn't go   d. didn't went

A: ___ **2.** "The water would ___ freezing at the beach!"

a. have   b. had been   c. being   d. have been

A: ___ **3.** The swimming pool is ___ the big park.

a. near   b. in front of   c. next to   d. behind

A: ___ **4.** Mary ___ to that swimming pool now.

a. going   b. is going   c. goes   d. gone

A: ___ **5.** Kevin ___ that swimming pool because the water is ___.

a. like, warm   b. likes, warm   c. like, cold   d. likes, cold

A: ___ **6.** Kevin ___ a movie last weekend.

a. saw   b. had seen   c. didn't see   d. didn't saw

A: ___ **7.** Kevin ___ a change of ___ about seeing a movie.

a. has, mind   b. had, mind   c. has, heart   d. had, heart

A: ___ **8.** Peter first walked around the ___.

a. supermarket   b. night market   c. beach   d. swimming pool

Answers on page 372

Lesson 6: Sports

спорт

What are you playing?

I am playing golf.

Learn the words

1. **basketball**
   баскетбол
2. **soccer**
   футбол
3. **badminton**
   бадминтон
4. **golf**
   гольф
5. **hockey**
   хоккей

6. **cricket**
   крикет
7. **tennis**
   теннис
8. **baseball**
   бейсбол
9. **volleyball**
   воллейбол
10. **football**
    футбол

Learn a verb

play – playing – played – played играть

Mary: I've been playing soccer since I was four years old.

Learn an idiom

A good sport

Meaning: Someone who can accept losing or be made fun of.

"We made fun of Johnny, but he was *a good sport* and laughed with us."

Jason: Hi, Mary. What are you doing today?

Mary: I'm playing badminton.

Jason: Who are you going to play with?

Mary: Susan is coming later. You can play with us if you like.

Jason: No, I can't. Kevin and Tom want to play tennis today.

Mary: I think tennis is more difficult than badminton.

Jason: I agree. Tennis needs a lot more practice.

Mary: That's true. Golf also is a really difficult sport.

Jason: I didn't know you played golf.

Mary: I've been having golf lessons for about twelve months.

Jason: I prefer team sports.

Mary: What's your favorite sport?

Jason: My favorite sport is volleyball.

Mary: Volleyball is fun, but I think soccer is better.

Jason: I'm not very good at soccer. I can't control the ball well.

Mary: That's surprising. You're an excellent basketball player.

Jason: I guess I'm not good at using my feet.

Mary: I've been playing soccer since I was four years old.

Jason: I saw you play soccer last Sunday. You scored three goals.

Mary: I remember that game. The other team wasn't very good.

Jason: Yes. They lost badly, but they were good sports.

Mary: Hey, there's Susan. I'll see you later.

Jason: Have fun playing badminton!

Unscramble the sentences

1. more / practice / lot / needs / a / Tennis

_____

2. golf / I / played / didn't / know / you

_____

3. tennis / I / think / than / difficult / more / badminton / is

_____

Answer the questions

1. Who is Mary going to play badminton with?

_____

2. What is Jason doing today?

_____

3. How long has Mary been having golf lessons?

_____

4. Which sport is Jason excellent at?

_____

5. How many goals did Mary score in the soccer game?

_____

Write the answer next to the letter "A"

A: ___ **1.** "I think tennis is ___ than badminton."

a. most difficult   b. more difficult   c. difficult   d. difficulter

A: ___ **2.** "I've been having golf lessons ___ about twelve months."

a. for   b. of   c. on   d. in

A: ___ **3.** Mary thinks golf is a ___ sport.

a. really difficult   b. real difficult   c. really easy   d. real easy

A: ___ **4.** Jason is not very ___ soccer.

a. good for   b. bad for   c. good at   d. bad at

A: ___ **5.** Did Mary score four goals at the soccer game last Sunday?

a. No, she don't.   b. Yes, she did.   c. No, she did.   d. No, she didn't.

A: ___ **6.** Mary ___ been playing soccer since she was four years old.

a. is   b. have   c. has   d. had

A: ___ **7.** Jason's favorite sport is ___.

a. basketball   b. volleyball   c. soccer   d. golf

A: ___ **8.** Jason can't control the ball ___.

a. well   b. good   c. badly   d. bad

Answers on page 372

Lesson 7: At the zoo

в зоопарке

> How many lions are there?
> There are two lions.

Learn the words

1. **monkey**
   обезьяна
2. **lion**
   лев
3. **tiger**
   тигр
4. **rhino**
   носорог
5. **bear**
   медведь

6. **penguin**
   пингвин
7. **giraffe**
   жираф
8. **elephant**
   слон
9. **kangaroo**
   кенгуру
10. **crocodile**
    крокодил

Learn a verb

like – liking – liked – liked любить, нравиться

Helen: That's right. I really like kangaroos. They are so amazing.

Learn an idiom

Let the cat out of the bag

Meaning: To let someone know a secret.

"He *let the cat out of the bag* about the surprise party."

Helen: Thanks for coming with me to the zoo today.

Emily: I love the zoo!

Helen: Me, too. I haven't been there for two years.

Emily: They have new animals now.

Helen: Really? Which new animals do they have?

Emily: I heard they have giraffes now.

Helen: How many giraffes do they have?

Emily: There are four giraffes. One of them is a baby giraffe.

Helen: That's so cute!

Emily: Last time I went, I thought the penguins were the cutest.

Helen: Are penguins your favorite animal?

Emily: No, my favorite animal is a lion. The zoo doesn't have any.

Helen: That's too bad.

Emily: Your favorite animal is a kangaroo, right?

Helen: That's right. I really like kangaroos. They are so amazing.

Emily: I didn't want to let the cat out of the bag, but guess what?

Helen: What?

Emily: There are two baby kangaroos at the zoo now.

Helen: Wow! I'm so excited to see them.

Emily: I wanted to make it a surprise and not tell you.

Helen: You know baby kangaroos are called joeys, right?

Emily: That's right! I forgot. Which animal should we see first?

Helen: The monkeys are funny. Let's go see them first.

Find the mistakes and write the sentence correctly

Emily: No, my favorite animal is a tiger. The zoo doesn't have any.

_____

Helen: The bears are funny. Let's go see them later.

_____

Emily: There are three giraffes. Two of them are baby giraffes.

_____

Answer the questions

1. Where are the girls going?

_____

2. What is Helen's favorite animal?

_____

3. Which animal does Emily think is the cutest?

_____

4. What are baby kangaroos called?

_____

5. Which animal does Helen think is funny?

_____

Write the answer next to the letter "A"

A: ___ **1.** Helen ___ to the zoo for two years.

a. haven't been   b. hasn't been   c. have been   d. has been

A: ___ **2.** There are four giraffes and one of ___ is a baby.

a. it   b. they   c. animal   d. them

A: ___ **3.** Emily thinks ___ are the cutest animals.

a. penguins   b. giraffes   c. monkeys   d. kangaroos

A: ___ **4.** The zoo ___ any lions.

a. doesn't have   b. don't have   c. have   d. has

A: ___ **5.** Helen thinks kangaroos ___.

a. amazing   b. is amazing   c. are amazing   d. amazingly

A: ___ **6.** Helen ___ likes kangaroos.

a. real   b. very   c. really   d. does

A: ___ **7.** Baby kangaroos ___ called ___.

a. is, joeys   b. is, joey   c. are, joey   d. are, joeys

A: ___ **8.** They want to see the monkeys ___.

a. first   b. last   c. later   d. now

Answers on page 372

Lesson 8: Colors

цвета

What is your favorite color?

My favorite color is red.

Learn the words

1. red
красный

2. blue
голубой

3. orange
оранжевый

4. pink
розовый

5. black
черный

6. yellow
желтый

7. green
зеленый

8. purple
лиловый

9. brown
коричневый

10. white
белый

Learn a verb

draw – drawing – drew – drawn рисовать

Susan: I'm not sure about what I should draw.

Learn an idiom

Feeling blue

Meaning: Feeling unhappy.

"He's *feeling blue* today because he lost the game."

Conversation

Susan: What are you drawing?

Jessica: I'm drawing my family.

Susan: Why do you want to draw your family?

Jessica: It's for Thanksgiving. I'm making a thank you card.

Susan: That's a great idea. Where did you get the pink paper?

Jessica: I bought it at the bookstore.

Susan: Is pink your favorite color?

Jessica: No, it isn't. My favorite color is purple.

Susan: Why didn't you buy purple paper?

Jessica: I wanted to, but the store didn't have any purple paper.

Susan: That's a shame.

Jessica: I'm feeling a little blue. I wanted to use purple paper.

Susan: Is that your mom? I didn't know she has black hair.

Jessica: She changed her hair color from brown a week ago.

Susan: I like her red dress. You draw really well.

Jessica: Thank you. I like to draw.

Susan: I'm not sure about what I should draw.

Jessica: What are you thankful for?

Susan: I really like our new house. Maybe I should draw that.

Jessica: You'll need a lot of different colors for the front yard.

Susan: I know! Mom planted a lot of colorful flowers.

Jessica: The yellow flowers are my favorite.

Susan: Mine, too. They are called carnations.

Put the sentences in order

Jessica: I'm drawing my family. ____

Susan: What are you drawing? ____

Jessica: No, it isn't. My favorite color is purple. ____

Susan: Is pink your favorite color? ____

Jessica: It's for Thanksgiving. I'm making a thank you card. ____

Susan: That's a great idea. Where did you get the pink paper? ____

Jessica: I bought it at the bookstore. ____

Susan: Why do you want to draw your family? ____

Answer the questions

1. What is Jessica drawing a picture of?

_____

2. What color paper did Jessica buy?

_____

3. Where did Jessica buy the paper at?

_____

4. What color hair did Jessica's mother have before?

_____

5. What is Susan thankful for?

_____

Write the answer next to the letter "A"

A: ___ **1.** Jessica is ___ a picture ___ her family.

a. draw, of   b. drawing, of   c. drawing, for   d. draws, for

A: ___ **2.** Susan ___ Jessica's thank you card is a great idea.

a. thought   b. think   c. thinking   d. thinks

A: ___ **3.** Did Jessica want to use pink paper?

a. No, she did.   b. No, she didn't.   c. Yes, she did.   d. No, she doesn't.

A: ___ **4.** Susan ___ know Jessica's mother has black hair.

a. isn't   b. don't   c. didn't   d. doesn't

A: ___ **5.** Susan thinks Jessica ___ very ___.

a. draw, well   b. draw, good   c. draws, well   d. draws, good

A: ___ **6.** Susan didn't know what ___.

a. to draw   b. will draw   c. draw   d. drawing

A: ___ **7.** Susan is thankful ___ her new house.

a. with   b. of   c. for   d. to

A: ___ **8.** Susan's mother planted ___ colorful flowers.

a. a lot   b. many   c. a few   d. a little

Answers on page 372

Lesson 9: Activities

занятия

> **What do you like to do?**
> **I like to read books.**

Learn the words

1. **play piano**
   играть на пианино
2. **read books**
   читать книги
3. **play video games**
   играть в видеоигры
4. **surf the internet**
   бродить по интернету
5. **take photos**
   снимать фотографии

6. **watch TV**
   смотреть ТВ
7. **sing songs**
   петь песни
8. **study English**
   изучать английский
9. **play cards**
   играть в карты
10. **go shopping**
    ходить за покупками

Learn a verb

read – reading – read – read читать

Matthew: I like to read books, but I'm feeling lazy. Let's watch TV.

Learn an idiom

Shop around

Meaning: To shop at different stores to find the best price.

"You should *shop around* before you buy this piano."

Matthew: What did you do last weekend?

John: I was playing video games.

Matthew: Which game were you playing?

John: I was playing the new hockey game.

Matthew: Awesome. I wanted to buy it, but it's too expensive.

John: You can shop around online. It's cheaper on the internet.

Matthew: Cool. I will surf the internet tonight.

John: What did you do last weekend?

Matthew: I studied English on Saturday.

John: Was that fun?

Matthew: Yes, it was. I like to study English.

John: Where do you study English?

Matthew: There's an English class I attend near the train station.

John: I know that place. My sister plays piano next door.

Matthew: I didn't know she plays piano.

John: She's been playing piano for three years.

Matthew: How about you?

John: I don't like to play piano. It's too difficult.

Matthew: What do you want to do now?

John: We can play cards or read books.

Matthew: I like to read books, but I'm feeling lazy. Let's watch TV.

John: Sure, but only for thirty minutes. I have to go shopping.

Matthew: That's fine. I have to take photos for art class later.

Fill in the blanks

Matthew: Which _____ were you _____?

John: I _____ playing the _____ hockey game.

John: What _____ you do _____ weekend?

Matthew: I _____ English _____ Saturday.

John: I know that _____. My sister plays _____ next door.

Matthew: I _____ know she _____ piano.

John: I _____ like to play piano. It's too _____.

Answer the questions

1. What was John doing last weekend?

_____

2. Why couldn't Matthew buy the hockey game?

_____

3. Where is Matthew's English class?

_____

4. How long has John's sister been playing piano?

_____

5. How long will they watch TV for?

_____

Write the answer next to the letter "A"

A: ___ **1.** Last weekend, John ___ playing video games.

a. are   b. is   c. were   d. was

A: ___ **2.** The hockey game is ___ to buy on the ___.

a. cheaper, internet b. cheap, online   c. expensive, internet   d. cheap, shop

A: ___ **3.** Matthew ___ the internet tonight.

a. surf   b. will surf   c. surfs   d. surfing

A: ___ **4.** Matthew attends an English class near the ___ station.

a. radio   b. police   c. fire   d. train

A: ___ **5.** John's sister has a piano class ___ to Matthew's English class.

a. near   b. by   c. next   d. beside

A: ___ **6.** Is playing piano too difficult for John?

a. Yes, it has.   b. Yes, it does.   c. Yes, it has been.   d. Yes, it is.

A: ___ **7.** What will John do after they watch TV?

a. Go shopping.   b. Play cards.   c. Read books.   d. Take photos.

A: ___ **8.** Which class does Matthew have to take photos for?

a. English class.   b. Piano class.   c. Art class.   d. History class.

Answers on page 372

Lesson 10: Food & Drinks

еда и напитки

How much tea is there?
There is a lot of tea.

Learn the words

1. **cake**
   пирожное
2. **cheese**
   сыр
3. **milk**
   молоко
4. **tea**
   чай
5. **soda**
   газировка

6. **pizza**
   пицца
7. **water**
   вода
8. **juice**
   сок
9. **coffee**
   кофе
10. **pie**
    пирог

Learn a verb

want – wanting – wanted – wanted хотеть

Helen: Do you want something to drink while we wait for the pizza?

Learn an idiom

Put food on the table

Meaning: To make money for the household expenses.

"I need this job to *put food on the table*."

Helen: What do you want to eat for lunch Kevin?

Kevin: I'm not sure. What do you have?

Helen: Let me check what's in the refrigerator.

Kevin: I haven't eaten all day, so I'm pretty hungry.

Helen: There's an apple pie in the refrigerator.

Kevin: Okay. How much pie is there?

Helen: There is only a little pie.

Kevin: Perhaps we should order a pizza. What do you think?

Helen: I think that's a good idea.

Kevin: What flavor pizza do you like?

Helen: I'm happy with a cheese pizza.

Kevin: That sounds good. Get some lemon soda as well.

Helen: We have some milk tea in the refrigerator.

Kevin: Oh, okay. Milk tea is fine. Is one pizza enough?

Helen: I think so. We have a chocolate cake for later.

Kevin: Was the cake baked by your mom?

Helen: Yes, it was.

Kevin: Your mom makes delicious cakes.

Helen: Do you want a drink while we wait for the pizza?

Kevin: Sure. Do you have any juice?

Helen: Sorry. Mom's working and hasn't gone shopping this week.

Kevin: No problem. Somebody has to put food on the table!

Helen: I'm starting to feel hungry now, too!

Unscramble the sentences

1. idea / a / that's / think / good / I

_____

2. have / later / We / cake / for / chocolate / a

_____

3. in / refrigerator / the / milk tea / We / some / have

_____

Answer the questions

1. Why is Kevin hungry?

_____

2. What flavor pizza did Helen order?

_____

3. What are they going to drink with the pizza?

_____

4. Who baked the chocolate cake?

_____

5. What does Kevin think about her mother's cakes?

_____

Write the answer next to the letter "A"

A: ___ **1.** Kevin ___ eaten all day, ___ he's pretty hungry.

a. haven't, and   b. hasn't, so   c. has, but   d. have, therefore

A: ___ **2.** There ___ an apple pie in the refrigerator.

a. was   b. have   c. had   d. were

A: ___ **3.** How ___ pie is ___ in the refrigerator?

a. much, that   b. many, there   c. much, there   d. many, here

A: ___ **4.** Who was happy with a cheese pizza?

a. Both children.   b. Helen.   c. Kevin.   d. Nobody.

A: ___ **5.** Did Helen order some lemon soda?

a. Yes, she is.   b. No, she didn't.   c. Yes, she does.   d. Yes, she did.

A: ___ **6.** Kevin ___ to drink lemon soda, but they had milk tea instead.

a. wants   b. want   c. wanted   d. wanting

A: ___ **7.** Helen's mother hasn't gone shopping because she is ___.

a. working   b. works   c. work   d. worked

A: ___ **8.** Helen's ___ puts ___ on the table in their family.

a. mother, money   b. father, money   c. father, food   d. mother, food

Answers on page 372

Lesson 11: At the fruit market

на фруктовом рынке

What do you want?

I want an apple.

Learn the words

1. **orange**
апельсин
2. **pear**
груша
3. **watermelon**
арбуз
4. **strawberry**
клубника
5. **cherry**
вишня

6. **lemon**
лимон
7. **banana**
банан
8. **grape**
виноград
9. **pineapple**
ананас
10. **apple**
яблоко

Learn a verb

need – needing – needed – needed нуждаться

Helen: There are two oranges, but I need them for tonight.

Learn an idiom

A bad apple

Meaning: The one bad person in a good group.

"He is *a bad apple* on this basketball team."

Tom: Hi, Helen. Did you just get home?

Helen: Hey, Tom. Yes, I just went shopping at the fruit market.

Tom: Wow! It looks like you got a lot of different things.

Helen: Yes, I'm going to prepare some fruit for dessert tonight.

Tom: Actually, I want to eat some fruit right now.

Helen: What do you want?

Tom: I want an apple. Is there an apple?

Helen: No, there isn't. The market didn't have any apples today.

Tom: I want an orange, then. Can I have an orange?

Helen: There are two oranges, but I need them for tonight.

Tom: That's okay. I'll wait until later. Who is coming tonight?

Helen: I invited John, Susan, and Emily.

Tom: Is Mary going to come for dinner, too?

Helen: I think she's a bad apple, so I didn't ask her.

Tom: Okay. What other fruit do you need for tonight?

Helen: I need a watermelon and two bananas.

Tom: Are there two bananas? I don't see any here.

Helen: Yes, they're under the grapes and the pears.

Tom: I don't want a pear. I like cherries more.

Helen: I bought a lemon and a pineapple, too.

Tom: Hmmm…There's only one other thing I need.

Helen: Oh? What do you need?

Tom: I need some strawberry ice cream.

Find the mistakes and write the sentence correctly

Helen: There are two apples, but I want them for tomorrow.

_____

Tom: Are there four pineapples? I don't have any there.

_____

Tom: I don't need a lemon. I like oranges better.

_____

Answer the questions

1. Where did Helen just go shopping?

_____

2. What is Helen going to prepare?

_____

3. Why didn't Helen buy any apples?

_____

4. Who did Helen invite for dinner?

_____

5. Where are the bananas?

_____

Write the answer next to the letter "A"

A: ___ **1.** Helen just went shopping at the ___.

a. supermarket   b. fruit market   c. night market   d. store

A: ___ **2.** Helen is going to prepare some ___ for dessert tonight.

a. ice cream   b. pie   c. fruit   d. cake

A: ___ **3.** Does Tom eat an orange?

a. Yes, he does.   b. No, he doesn't.   c. Yes, he can.   d. No, he isn't.

A: ___ **4.** How many apples did Helen buy today?

a. None.   b. One.   c. Two.   d. Three.

A: ___ **5.** Helen thinks Mary is a bad ___.

a. grape   b. pineapple   c. orange   d. apple

A: ___ **6.** Tom doesn't see any ___.

a. cherries   b. grapes   c. pears   d. bananas

A: ___ **7.** Tom likes ___ better than pears.

a. cherries   b. grapes   c. pineapples   d. lemons

A: ___ **8.** What kind of dessert did Tom want?

a. Grapes.   b. Strawberries.   c. Ice cream.   d. Cherries.

Answers on page 372

Lesson 12: Shapes

фигуры

> What color is this circle?
>
> This is a green circle.

Learn the words

1. **square**
   квадрат
2. **circle**
   круг
3. **star**
   звезда
4. **heart**
   сердце
5. **octagon**
   восьмиугольник

6. **triangle**
   треугольник
7. **rectangle**
   прямоугольник
8. **oval**
   овал
9. **diamond**
   ромб
10. **pentagon**
    пятиугольник

Learn a verb

find – finding – found – found находить

Jason: I'm doing homework. I have to find shapes in this picture.

Learn an idiom

Be out of shape

Meaning: To be unfit or overweight.

"He can't climb this mountain. He *is* really *out of shape*!"

Susan: What are you doing right now?

Jason: I'm doing homework. I have to find shapes in this picture.

Susan: What do you mean?

Jason: For example, this table is a blue oval.

Susan: Oh, I see! This stop sign is a red octagon!

Jason: That's right, and this painting is a green square.

Susan: Interesting! Look at this clock. Is this circle white?

Jason: No, it isn't. It's yellow. You're good at finding shapes.

Susan: It's pretty fun. What color is that door?

Jason: That door is a brown rectangle. Nice work!

Susan: What other homework do you have to do?

Jason: Well, I also have to draw some shapes and colors.

Susan: It says that you have to draw a heart and a star.

Jason: Those are easy, but I'm not very good at drawing.

Susan: That's because you like sports more than homework.

Jason: Well, I don't want to be out of shape.

Susan: Yes, but you also need to finish your homework on time.

Jason: Just help me find a diamond and a pentagon.

Susan: Okay, and then we can go outside. It's a sunny day.

Jason: I'll do this quickly, so then we can go to the park.

Susan: Wait, is this triangle black?

Jason: Yes, it is. Now, you're finding all of my mistakes.

Susan: Let's make sure you do it right.

Put the sentences in order

Jason: That door is a brown rectangle. Nice work! ____

Jason: Those are easy, but I'm not very good at drawing. ____

Susan: What other homework do you have to do? ____

Jason: Well, I don't want to be out of shape. ____

Susan: It's pretty fun. What color is that door? ____

Susan: It says that you have to draw a heart and a star. ____

Jason: Well, I also have to draw some shapes and colors. ____

Susan: That's because you like sports more than homework. ____

Answer the questions

1. What is Jason doing now?

_____

2. What shape is the table?

_____

3. What does Jason have to draw?

_____

4. Where do they want to go?

_____

5. How is the weather?

_____

Write the answer next to the letter "A"

A: ___ **1.** Jason ___ to find shapes in the picture.

a. have   b. got   c. is   d. has

A: ___ **2.** The stop sign is a red ___.

a. octagon   b. circle   c. oval   d. pentagon

A: ___ **3.** Does Jason have other homework to do?

a. Yes, he will.   b. Yes, he does.   c. No, he won't.   d. No, he doesn't.

A: ___ **4.** Jason ___ very good at drawing.

a. doesn't   b. can't   c. isn't   d. hasn't

A: ___ **5.** Susan says he ___ sports more than drawing.

a. finds   b. liking   c. likes   d. like

A: ___ **6.** Jason doesn't want to be out of ___.

a. color   b. shape   c. oval   d. homework

A: ___ **7.** Susan is ___ all of Jason's mistakes.

a. finding   b. found   c. looking   d. look

A: ___ **8.** The ___ is ___.

a. heart, red   b. circle, white   c. square, blue   d. triangle, black

Answers on page 372

Lesson 13: At the supermarket

в супермаркете

What do you want to buy?
I want to buy some bread.

Learn the words

1. **milk**
   молоко
2. **juice**
   сок
3. **meat**
   мясо
4. **drinks**
   напитки
5. **vegetables**
   овощи

6. **ice cream**
   мороженое
7. **fruit**
   фрукт
8. **bread**
   хлеб
9. **fish**
   рыба
10. **pizza**
    пицца

Learn a verb

get – getting – got – gotten получать

Max: No, I got some pizza yesterday.

Learn an idiom

A rip off

Meaning: Something is too expensive.

"The supermarket around the corner is *a rip off*."

Max: I love shopping at different supermarkets.

Julie: You really like going out to buy different food and drinks.

Max: Yes, I like to shop around for the lowest prices.

Julie: I hope I can help. What do you want to buy first?

Max: First, I want to buy some vegetables.

Julie: Do you want to buy some fruit, too?

Max: No, I don't want to buy any fruit here.

Julie: Oh? Why don't you want to buy any fruit?

Max: The fruit at this place is a rip off!

Julie: Okay, so you'll buy fruit at the next place?

Max: Yes, that's right. I also want to buy some bread.

Julie: That sounds good. Do you want to get some pizza?

Max: No, I got some pizza yesterday.

Julie: What else do you want to buy from here?

Max: I want to buy some fish and some meat.

Julie: Do you also want to buy some juice or drinks?

Max: I would like some drinks. I don't need any juice.

Julie: I also see some ice cream and milk over there.

Max: I don't want anything sweet, so I don't want any ice cream.

Julie: Do you want to buy some milk?

Max: No, I don't. I know a better place to buy milk.

Julie: You really are a good shopper. You know all the best places.

Max: Well, eating is one of my favorite hobbies!

Fill in the blanks

Max: First, I want to _____ some _____.

Julie: _____ you want to buy some _____, too?

Max: No, I _____ want to buy _____ fruit here.

Julie: Oh? _____ don't you _____ to buy any fruit?

Max: The fruit at this _____ is a rip _____!

Julie: Okay, so _____ buy fruit at the _____ place?

Max: Yes, that's _____. I also want to buy some _____.

Answer the questions

1. What does Max love doing?

_____

2. Does Max want to buy some fruit?

_____

3. When did Max buy some pizza?

_____

4. What is one of Max's favorite hobbies?

_____

5. Why doesn't Max want ice cream?

_____

Write the answer next to the letter "A"

A: ___ **1.** Max really ___ going out to ___ food and drinks.

a. likes, buys   b. like, get   c. like, eat   d. likes, buy

A: ___ **2.** Max shops ___ for the lowest prices.

a. off   b. on   c. over   d. around

A: ___ **3.** Julie asked Max if he wanted to buy ___.

a. fish   b. fruit   c. meat   d. bread

A: ___ **4.** They didn't buy ___ because it was a rip ___.

a. bread, over   b. fruit, off   c. pizza, around   d. juice, on

A: ___ **5.** When did Max get pizza?

a. Last week.   b. First.   c. Yesterday.   d. On Monday.

A: ___ **6.** Max also wanted to buy some ___ and ___.

a. bread, juice   b. pizza, milk   c. vegetables, ice cream   d. fish, meat

A: ___ **7.** Max said he knew a ___ place to buy milk.

a. better   b. favorite   c. sweet   d. cheaper

A: ___ **8.** What did Max say was one of his favorite hobbies?

a. Buying.   b. Shopping.   c. Eating.   d. Getting.

Answers on page 372

Lesson 14: At the ice cream shop

в магазине мороженого

Which flavor do you like?

I like mint flavor.

Learn the words

1. **chocolate**
   шоколадное
2. **strawberry**
   клубничное
3. **mint**
   мятное
4. **raspberry**
   малиновое
5. **cherry**
   вишневое

6. **vanilla**
   ванильное
7. **coffee**
   кофейное
8. **almond**
   миндальное
9. **caramel**
   карамельное
10. **coconut**
    кокосовое

Learn a verb

have/has – having – had – had иметь

John: My friend said that the ice cream shop has many flavors.

Learn an idiom

Flavor of the month

Meaning: Something is suddenly popular for a short time.

"This song is just the *flavor of the month*."

Bob: I went out with my brother last Tuesday to play volleyball.

John: That sounds fun. Where did you go to play?

Bob: After lunch, we went to the beach with some friends.

John: How many people went with you?

Bob: There were five people. My sister came with us, too.

John: I'm surprised your sister likes to play volleyball.

Bob: I think volleyball is just the flavor of the month for her.

John: What do you mean?

Bob: She'll like it for a short time, and then she'll change.

John: Ok. I also heard about a new ice cream shop near the beach.

Bob: Yes, we went there later. It's a small place beside a gym.

John: My friend said that the ice cream shop has many flavors.

Bob: Yes, it was really hard to choose. We all had different flavors.

John: Which flavor does your brother like?

Bob: He likes raspberry, but doesn't like cherry flavor.

John: That's interesting. Does your sister like the same flavors?

Bob: No, she doesn't. She likes caramel, almond and coffee.

John: Does the shop have chocolate, vanilla and strawberry?

Bob: Yes, it does. It also has mint and coconut. It's great.

John: Now, I really want to go there. I feel like having ice cream.

Bob: Me, too. Actually, I think I like ice cream a little too much.

John: Oh? So, which flavor do you like?

Bob: Well, it was too hard to choose, so I had every flavor.

Unscramble the sentences

1. like / brother / does / flavor / your / Which

_____

2. likes / and / coffee / caramel / She / almond

_____

3. little / think / much / I / a / I / cream / ice / like / too

_____

Answer the questions

1. Which day did they go to the beach?

_____

2. Who did they go to the beach with?

_____

3. Where is the ice cream shop?

_____

4. What does John feel like having now?

_____

5. What flavor did Bob have?

_____

Write the answer next to the letter "A"

A: ___ **1.** They went to the beach last ___ to play volleyball.

a. weekend   b. Tuesday   c. night   d. lunch

A: ___ **2.** ___ people went with them.

a. four   b. five   c. family   d. beach

A: ___ **3.** Bob thinks volleyball is the ___ of the ___ for his sister.

a. taste, month   b. play, day   c. flavor, month   d. taste, day

A: ___ **4.** John ___ there is a ___ ice cream shop near the beach.

a. saw, different   b. thinks, fun   c. read, flavor   d. heard, new

A: ___ **5.** Who said there were many different flavors?

a. Kevin.   b. Bob.   c. John.   d. Bob's brother.

A: ___ **6.** His brother likes ___, but doesn't like ___ flavor.

a. raspberry, cherry b. cherry, raspberry c. caramel, cherry d. mint, coconut

A: ___ **7.** ___ thinks he ___ ice cream a little too much.

a. Bob, like   b. John, eats   c. Bob, likes   d. Bob's sister, has

A: ___ **8.** Bob said it ___ hard to ___ a flavor.

a. is, chosen   b. has, choice   c. was, choosing   d. was, choose

Answers on page 372

Lesson 15: In the refrigerator

в холодильнике

What do you want to eat?

I want to eat rice.

Learn the words

1. **rice**
   рис
2. **salad**
   салад
3. **toast**
   тост
4. **soup**
   суп
5. **dumplings**
   пельмениа

6. **tea**
   чай
7. **cola**
   кола
8. **eggs**
   яйца
9. **water**
   вода
10. **ice**
    лед

Learn a verb

sell – selling – sold – sold продавать

Peter: A man was selling them at the night market last night.

Learn an idiom

Be as cold as ice

Meaning: To describe someone who is very unfriendly.

"The teacher *was as cold as ice* after she caught me cheating on the science test."

Conversation

Peter: That was a really fun soccer game this morning.

Mary: Yes, the weather today was great. It wasn't too hot.

Peter: I think Emily wasn't happy when you scored against her.

Mary: Yeah, after the game she was as cold as ice.

Peter: I called her after we got home. She'll be fine.

Mary: Are you hungry? What do you want to eat?

Peter: I don't want to eat anything hot, like soup.

Mary: I think we have other things. What's in the refrigerator?

Peter: We have rice, eggs, and dumplings.

Mary: Where did you get the dumplings from?

Peter: A man was selling them at the night market last night.

Mary: Do you want to eat dumplings?

Peter: No, I don't. I ate them last night. Do you want to eat toast?

Mary: No, I don't want to eat toast. Maybe I'll just have salad.

Peter: What do you want to drink?

Mary: I want to drink tea or cola. Do we have ice?

Peter: Yes, we have ice. I don't want to drink anything sweet.

Mary: There's water. Do you want to drink water?

Peter: Yes, I do. I need to drink water after playing sports today.

Mary: Your brother is at home too. What does he want to drink?

Peter: He doesn't like tea or soda. Maybe he wants to drink juice.

Mary: I'll ask him if he wants water, juice, or milk.

Peter: Wow! It's really difficult to get food and drinks for everyone.

Find the mistakes and write the sentence correctly

Peter: A boy was selling them at the cinema last night.

_____

Mary: No, I don't want to eat meat. Maybe I'll just have candy.

_____

Peter: He doesn't like milk or cola. Maybe she wants to drink tea.

_____

Answer the questions

1. When did they play soccer?

_____

2. What does Peter not want to eat?

_____

3. Where did Peter get the dumplings from?

_____

4. What does Mary want to drink?

_____

5. Who was as cold as ice?

_____

Write the answer next to the letter "A"

A: ___ **1.** The weather was ___. It wasn't too ___.

a. hot, great   b. ice, cold   c. fun, hot   d. great, hot

A: ___ **2.** Emily wasn't ___ after the game.

a. hungry   b. friendly   c. eating   d. drinking

A: ___ **3.** Peter didn't want to eat anything ___.

a. cold   b. ice   c. difficult   d. hot

A: ___ **4.** He got the ___ at the night market.

a. dumplings   b. eggs   c. rice   d. toast

A: ___ **5.** Mary ___ want to eat toast.

a. don't   b. did   c. doesn't   d. do

A: ___ **6.** Peter needs to drink water after ___.

a. eating   b. dumplings   c. playing sports   d. selling

A: ___ **7.** Peter's brother doesn't like ___ or ___.

a. tea, soda   b. tea, juice   c. water, milk   d. soda, juice

A: ___ **8.** Peter said it's ___ to get food and drinks for everyone.

a. fun   b. difficult   c. great   d. sweet

Answers on page 372

Lesson 16: Jobs

работа

What is her job?

She is a salesclerk.

Learn the words

1. **doctor**
   врач
2. **cook**
   повар
3. **nurse**
   медсестра, медбрат
4. **police officer**
   полицейский
5. **taxi driver**
   таксист

6. **teacher**
   учитель
7. **farmer**
   фермер
8. **salesclerk**
   продавец
9. **firefighter**
   пожарный
10. **builder**
   строитель

Learn a verb

work – working – worked – worked работать

John: My aunt has a job working with food. She loves it.

Learn an idiom

Keep up the good work

Meaning: To encourage someone to keep doing well.

"You're doing a great job. *Keep up the good work.*"

Sam: I saw Matthew's father working yesterday in the city.

John: You saw his father? What's his job?

Sam: He's a police officer. He was driving a police car.

John: I thought his father was a firefighter. Is he a firefighter, too?

Sam: No, he was before, but he changed jobs.

John: I told the teacher I want to have a good job in the future.

Sam: Me too. He said to study, and to keep up the good work.

John: I think I want to be a doctor or a nurse.

Sam: You'll have to study hard. I want a job working with food.

John: My aunt has a job working with food. She loves it.

Sam: Is she a cook?

John: No, she isn't. She's a farmer. She sells many vegetables.

Sam: My brother has a job selling things right now, too.

John: Is he a salesclerk?

Sam: Yes, he is, but he wants to get a job as a builder this fall.

John: Mary's parents were builders before. Now they drive.

Sam: Are they taxi drivers?

John: Yes, they are. They work very hard every day.

Sam: I guess that's why Mary doesn't have to walk anywhere.

John: I think the important thing is to get a job that's interesting.

Sam: I agree. I don't want to feel bored at my job.

John: Maybe you should play video games less and study more.

Sam: That's probably a good idea. I'll start after this game!

Put the sentences in order

Sam: You should study hard. I want a job working with food. ____

Sam: My brother has a job selling things right now, too. ____

Sam: Is she a cook? ____

John: Is he a salesclerk? ____

John: I think I want to be a doctor or a nurse. ____

John: My aunt has a job working with food. She loves it. ____

Sam: Yes, he is, but he wants to get a job as a builder. ____

John: No, she isn't. She's a farmer. She sells vegetables. ____

Answer the questions

1. What is Matthew's father's job?

_____

2. What did John tell the teacher?

_____

3. Who has an aunt that works with food?

_____

4. What were Mary's parents before?

_____

5. Why does Sam want an interesting job?

_____

Write the answer next to the letter "A"

A: ___ **1.** Sam saw Matthew's father ___.

a. today   b. yesterday   c. this morning   d. Tuesday

A: ___ **2.** Matthew's father was ___ a police car.

a. drive   b. drove   c. drives   d. driving

A: ___ **3.** The teacher said to keep ___ the good work.

a. up   b. on   c. in   d. over

A: ___ **4.** John's ___ has a job ___ with food.

a. aunt, working   b. mother, cooking   c. uncle, work   d. father, selling

A: ___ **5.** Sam's ___ has a job ___ things.

a. aunt, working   b. brother, selling   c. father, driving   d. aunt, farming

A: ___ **6.** ___ parents work very hard every day.

a. Sam   b. Sam's   c. Mary's   d. Mary

A: ___ **7.** Who wants to get a job that's interesting?

a. Sam's aunt.   b. Matthew.   c. Mary.   d. John.

A: ___ **8.** Who should play video games less and study more?

a. John.   b. Mary.   c. Sam.   d. John's brother.

Answers on page 372

Lesson 17: Names

имена

> **What's her name?**
> **Her name is Helen.**

Learn the words

1. John
Джон

2. Matthew
Мэттью

3. Jason
Джейсон

4. Helen
Хелен

5. Mary
Мэри

6. Kevin
Кевин

7. Tom
Том

8. Emily
Эмили

9. Jessica
Джессика

10. Susan
Сьюзан

Learn a verb

call – calling – called – called звонить

Kevin: Sure, and we can also call some old friends to meet us.

Learn an idiom

A household name

Meaning: To describe someone famous who everyone knows.

"The actor became *a household name* after he won an Oscar for his performance."

Kevin: Hey, what are you doing right now?

Ted: I'm looking at some old pictures of friends and family.

Kevin: That's interesting. Is this for homework?

Ted: It isn't homework. I just like things from a long time ago.

Kevin: Where did you find them? There are so many pictures.

Ted: I found an old box upstairs after I came home from the gym.

Kevin: This guy looks like you, but older. What's his name?

Ted: That's my uncle. His name is Jason. His friends call him J.

Kevin: The woman beside him, is her name Emily?

Ted: That's right, it's my Aunt Emily. She's my uncle's wife.

Kevin: Who's this other guy that's playing the piano?

Ted: That's another uncle. He was a household name before.

Kevin: He was a famous singer, right? What's his name?

Ted: His name is John. He wasn't a singer, he was a famous cook.

Kevin: Hey, here's our old school photo too.

Ted: This girl in the front, what's her name?

Kevin: Her name's Susan, she's at a different school now.

Ted: There's Tom, Helen, Mary, and Jessica. We look so young!

Kevin: Hey, look at the time. We should get something to eat.

Ted: Do you want to go to a restaurant for dinner?

Kevin: Sure, and we can also call some old friends to meet us.

Ted: Okay. Where do you want to go eat?

Kevin: How about your famous uncle cooks for us?

Fill in the blanks

Kevin: The woman _____ him, is her _____ Emily?

Ted: _____ right, it's my Aunt Emily. She's my _____ wife.

Kevin: Who's this _____ guy that's playing the _____?

Ted: That's another _____. He was a _____ name before.

Kevin: He was a _____ singer? _____ his name?

Ted: _____ name is John. He was a famous _____.

Kevin: Hey, _____'s our old _____ photo too.

Answer the questions

1. What is Ted doing right now?

_____

2. Where did he find the box of old pictures?

_____

3. When did he find the box?

_____

4. What did they call his uncle John before?

_____

5. What was the girl's name in the front of the school photo?

_____

Write the answer next to the letter "A"

A: ___ **1.** Ted is looking at pictures of ___ and ___.

a. friends, family   b. animals, friends   c. aunts, uncles   d. sisters, brothers

A: ___ **2.** Are the pictures a part of Ted's homework?

a. No, they didn't.   b. Yes, they are.   c. Yes, they can.   d. No, they aren't.

A: ___ **3.** He ___ the pictures in an ___ box upstairs.

a. found, old   b. saw, orange   c. bought, open   d. got, ugly

A: ___ **4.** Before he looked at the pictures, he was at the ___.

a. school   b. restaurant   c. gym   d. household

A: ___ **5.** The person who looks like Ted is his ___.

a. father   b. aunt   c. uncle   d. grandfather

A: ___ **6.** Uncle John ___ a singer, he was a ___ cook.

a. was, great   b. wasn't, famous   c. isn't, bad   d. couldn't, household

A: ___ **7.** They want to go to a ___ and eat ___.

a. store, dinner   b. restaurant, dinner   c. park, lunch   d. school, snacks

A: ___ **8.** Who did Kevin want to call to meet them?

a. A famous singer.   b. Aunt Emily.   c. Old friends.   d. Old uncles.

Answers on page 372

Lesson 18: More places

еще места

Where did you go yesterday?

I went to school.

Learn the words

1. **the library**
   библиотека
2. **school**
   школа
3. **the hospital**
   больница
4. **the train station**
   железнодорожная станция
5. **the police station**
   полицейский участок

6. **the office**
   офис
7. **the factory**
   завод, фабрика
8. **the clinic**
   клиника
9. **the bus stop**
   автобусная остановка
10. **the fire station**
    пожарное депо

Learn a verb

go – going – went – gone идти, ходить

Kevin: Yeah, she wasn't feeling well, so she went to a clinic.

Learn an idiom

Heart is in the right place

Meaning: To mean well and try to do the right thing.

"He makes a lot of mistakes, but his *heart is in the right place*."

Jessica: Hi, Kevin. I saw your sister last week at the bus stop.

Kevin: Yeah, she wasn't feeling well, so she went to a clinic.

Jessica: She didn't look very well, and she was coughing.

Kevin: Later, she wasn't feeling better, so we went to the hospital.

Jessica: Is she okay? I heard that many people are sick now.

Kevin: Yes, I was in the library on Monday and it was empty.

Jessica: Maybe I should bring your sister some soup.

Kevin: Well, your heart is in the right place, but I think she's fine.

Jessica: It's okay. On my way to the office, I'll go to her house.

Kevin: That's very nice. There's a good soup place near the school.

Jessica: How are you feeling? You look a bit tired.

Kevin: This week was really busy. I had to go to many places.

Jessica: Where did you go yesterday?

Kevin: I went to the train station. I had to meet my aunt.

Jessica: Is she the one who works at the police station?

Kevin: Yes, that's right. Then we went to the factory.

Jessica: Why did you go to the factory?

Kevin: Her friend works there, so she wanted to say hello.

Jessica: It really sounds like you had a busy week!

Kevin: Yes, I think I've gone to almost every place I know.

Jessica: Did you also go to the fire station yesterday?

Kevin: How did you know that we went to the fire station, too?

Jessica: Well, it's the only place in the city you didn't say yet.

Unscramble the sentences

1. go / did / yesterday / you / Where

_____

2. the / Is / at / one / the / works / who / she / police / station

_____

3. to / you / go / the / yesterday / also / station / Did / fire

_____

Answer the questions

1. When did Jessica see Kevin's sister?

_____

2. Who wasn't feeling well last week?

_____

3. When was Kevin at the library?

_____

4. Where is a good place to get soup?

_____

5. Why did Kevin go to the train station?

_____

Write the answer next to the letter "A"

A: ___ **1.** Last week, Kevin's sister was at the ___.

a. bus stop   b. library   c. school   d. police station

A: ___ **2.** Jessica's heart is in the right ___.

a. beat   b. clinic   c. place   d. feeling

A: ___ **3.** Jessica heard many people are ___ right now.

a. well   b. coughing   c. empty   d. sick

A: ___ **4.** When Kevin's sister wasn't feeling better, she went to the ___.

a. school   b. library   c. hospital   d. bus stop

A: ___ **5.** Kevin's ___ was really ___.

a. sister, tired   b. month, sick   c. day, tired   d. week, busy

A: ___ **6.** Kevin and his ___ went to the ___.

a. sister, school   b. aunt, factory   c. brother, bus stop   d. aunt, clinic

A: ___ **7.** Kevin's ___ works at the ___.

a. aunt, factory   b. aunt, police station   c. sister, clinic   d. sister, library

A: ___ **8.** Did Kevin and his aunt go to the fire station?

a. Yes, they did.   b. Yes, the will.   c. No, they didn't.   d. No, they won't.

Answers on page 372

Lesson 19: Meats

мясо

What did he eat for lunch?

He ate chicken.

Learn the words

1. beef
говядина

2. pork
свинина

3. bacon
бекон

4. fish
рыба

5. salami
салями

6. chicken
курица

7. lamb
баранина

8. ham
ветчина

9. sausage
колбаса, сосиски

10. shrimp
креветка

Learn a verb

eat – eating – ate – eaten есть

Matthew: Yes, I want to start eating well and doing more exercise.

Learn an idiom

Beef up

Meaning: To strengthen something or somebody.

"We need to *beef up* our efforts if we are going to do well this year."

Helen: Hi, Matthew. You've been looking very healthy recently.

Matthew: Yes, I want to start eating well and do more exercise.

Helen: I didn't know you enjoyed sports and exercise.

Matthew: Yes, my new plan is to go to the gym and beef up.

Helen: So, you'll need to eat well, too. What did you eat for lunch?

Matthew: I ate well! I didn't eat salami or sausage. I ate chicken.

Helen: If you want to eat meat, I have lots at home.

Matthew: So, you like to eat meat. Did you have pork for lunch?

Helen: Yes, I did. I also ate ham and bacon for breakfast.

Matthew: That's a lot of meat. Maybe you can try eating a salad.

Helen: Oh, I ate some vegetables, too. I like eating a lot.

Matthew: What did you eat for dinner?

Helen: For dinner, I ate lamb and fish. I didn't eat beef.

Matthew: Why didn't you eat beef?

Helen: Well, I wanted to eat some cake for dessert.

Matthew: Wow. You really eat a lot of food every day.

Helen: Yes, that's right. Oh! I also ate shrimp as a snack last night.

Matthew: If you're eating this much food, how can you be healthy?

Helen: I didn't say I was healthy, I just said I like eating.

Matthew: Maybe you and I should try playing sports sometime.

Helen: That's a good idea, but I'm not sure I can.

Matthew: Why not? I think it's a good idea to be in shape.

Helen: I need lots of time to buy food at the supermarket.

Find the mistakes and write the sentence correctly

Matthew: Yes, I want to start eating more and doing less exercise.

_____

Helen: Yes, I did. I also ate fish and salad for lunch.

_____

Helen: Well, I wanted to eat some beef for dinner.

_____

Answer the questions

1. What is Matthew's new plan?

_____

2. When did Matthew eat chicken?

_____

3. Why didn't Helen eat beef?

_____

4. Who ate shrimp as a snack last night?

_____

5. Where does Helen buy her food at?

_____

Write the answer next to the letter "A"

A: ___ **1.** Matthew ___ been looking very healthy recently.

a. have   b. having   c. has   d. was

A: ___ **2.** Helen didn't know he enjoyed ___ and ___.

a. sports, exercise   b. beef, salami   c. gym, chicken   d. ham, breakfast

A: ___ **3.** Matthew didn't eat ___ and ___ for lunch.

a. ham, bacon   b. lamb, fish   c. salami, sausage   d. beef, salad

A: ___ **4.** Helen has lots of ___ in her refrigerator.

a. salad   b. meat   c. pork   d. shrimp

A: ___ **5.** Helen didn't eat ___ because she wanted ___.

a. sausage, chicken   b. salami, chicken   c. lamb, fish   d. beef, cake

A: ___ **6.** When did Helen eat shrimp?

a. For breakfast.   b. For dinner.   c. Every day.   d. Last night.

A: ___ **7.** Helen said she likes ___.

a. eating   b. supermarkets   c. being healthy   d. playing sports

A: ___ **8.** Matthew ___ Helen really ___ a lot of food.

a. saying, ate   b. thinking, eating   c. think, eat   d. thinks, eats

Answers on page 372

Lesson 20: Vegetables

овощи

> What will you cook tonight?
>
> I will cook pumpkin.

Learn the words

1. **pumpkin**
тыква
2. **potato**
картофель
3. **carrot**
морковь
4. **asparagus**
спаржа
5. **broccoli**
брокколи

6. **corn**
кукуруза
7. **cabbage**
капуста
8. **spinach**
шпинат
9. **mushroom**
гриб
10. **onion**
лук

Learn a verb

cook – cooking – cooked – cooked готовить пищу

Mary: Yes, my sister is cooking a big meal tomorrow night.

Learn an idiom

Carrot on a stick

Meaning: A reward that is promised upon completion of a task.

"The coach gave his players a *carrot on a stick* and promised to take them all out for dinner if they win the game."

Tom: Wow! You really like to go shopping. That's a lot of stuff.

Mary: Yes, my sister is cooking a big meal tomorrow night.

Tom: What will she cook tomorrow?

Mary: We all like vegetables, so she'll cook mushrooms.

Tom: Will she only cook mushrooms?

Mary: No, she will also cook pumpkin, broccoli, and corn.

Tom: I see you also bought asparagus and cabbage.

Mary: Yes, she is really good at cooking. Hey, you should come!

Tom: I'm not sure if I can. I have to study English.

Mary: Emily will be there, and I know you like her.

Tom: You're just using her as a carrot on a stick, so I'll go.

Mary: Well, there will also be lots of great food.

Tom: Will your sister cook spinach? I love spinach.

Mary: Of course. She will also cook potato and carrot.

Tom: That's a lot. What won't she cook tomorrow?

Mary: She won't cook onion because it makes her cry.

Tom: If I don't go, I think I'll also cry. It sounds really great.

Mary: If you want to, you can bring some drinks.

Tom: Okay. I'll bring some juice, tea, and soda. How's that?

Mary: Good. Maybe also bring some fruit, meat, and ice cream.

Tom: Alright. Do you need anything else for this dinner?

Mary: Also, we need a little music, so you should play piano.

Tom: Wow! It sounds more like I'm the one having the party.

Put the sentences in order

Tom: I'm not sure if I can. I have to study English. ____

Mary: No, she will also cook pumpkin, broccoli, and corn. ____

Mary: We all like vegetables, so she'll cook mushrooms. ____

Mary: Emily will be there, and I know you like her. ____

Tom: I see you also bought asparagus and cabbage. ____

Mary: Yes, she is really good at cooking. You should come! ____

Tom: What will she cook tomorrow? ____

Tom: Will she only cook mushrooms? ____

Answer the questions

1. Who will cook a big meal tomorrow night?

_____

2. Why won't she cook onion?

_____

3. What did Mary also buy?

_____

4. Why is Tom not sure if he can go?

_____

5. What vegetables will she cook?

_____

Write the answer next to the letter "A"

A: ___ **1.** Mary really ___ to go ___ .

a. like, cooking   b. likes, cook   c. likes, shopping   d. like, shopping

A: ___ **2.** Her sister is cooking a big meal ___ .

a. tomorrow night   b. tonight   c. on Monday   d. today

A: ___ **3.** Will she only cook mushrooms?

a. Yes, she will.   b. No, they can't.   c. No, she won't.   d. Yes, they cook.

A: ___ **4.** Mary also ___ asparagus.

a. shopped   b. cooked   c. fought   d. bought

A: ___ **5.** Tom loves ___ .

a. Emily   b. spinach   c. potato   d. English

A: ___ **6.** She won't cook ___ because it makes her ___ .

a. carrot, sad   b. onion, cry   c. onion, study   d. carrot, stick

A: ___ **7.** Tom said he'll ___ some drinks.

a. need   b. drink   c. buy   d. bring

A: ___ **8.** Mary said Tom should ___ the ___ .

a. play, piano   b. find, drinks   c. bring, piano   d. cook, meat

Answers on page 372

Lesson 21: At school

в школе

> Where is the art room?
> The art room is next to the gym.

Learn the words

1. **classroom**
   класс, классная комната
2. **office**
   офис, кабинет
3. **nurse's office**
   медпункт
4. **gym**
   спортзал
5. **hall**
   зал

6. **computer lab**
   компьютерный класс
7. **art room**
   класс искусств
8. **music room**
   музыкальный класс
9. **science lab**
   класс естественных наук
10. **lunchroom**
    столовая

Learn a verb

put – putting – put – put ложить, ставить

Peter: I thought I had put it in the classroom, but it's not there.

Learn an idiom

Old school

Meaning: To do something the old-fashioned way.

"We're going to do this *old school* and use a hammer."

Peter: Hey, Mary. Have you seen my towel?

Mary: No, I haven't. Why do you need it?

Peter: I have a swimming class at the gym today.

Mary: When did you last see it?

Peter: I thought I had put it in the classroom, but it's not there.

Mary: I saw you in the lunchroom this morning. Maybe it's there.

Peter: No, I checked.

Mary: What color is the towel?

Peter: It's yellow and blue.

Mary: I remember seeing a yellow and blue towel in the art room.

Peter: That's strange. Where is the art room?

Mary: It's across from the nurse's office. Why is that strange?

Peter: I don't take any art classes, so I don't go to the art room.

Mary: That is strange. Maybe that towel I saw isn't yours.

Peter: I really hope I can find it. My class starts in ten minutes.

Mary: Usually, people put lost property in the office.

Peter: Which one? There are two offices at this school.

Mary: The one next to the science lab.

Peter: Is that the office where Mr. Miller works?

Mary: Yes, that's the one.

Peter: He's old school. You must knock on his door before entering.

Mary: Hey, Peter. What's that blue thing sticking out of your bag?

Peter: Ha! That's my towel. I'm so embarrassed.

Learn the English

Fill in the blanks

Mary: When _____ you _____ see it?

Peter: I _____ I had put it in the _____, but it's not there.

Mary: That is strange. _____ that towel I saw isn't _____.

Peter: _____ one? There are two _____ at this school.

Mary: Usually, people put lost _____ in the _____.

Peter: Is that the office _____ Mr. Miller _____?

Mary: Yes, _____ the _____.

Answer the questions

1. What is Peter looking for?

_____

2. Why does Peter need a towel?

_____

3. Where did Mary see Peter this morning?

_____

4. Where is the art room?

_____

5. When does Peter's swimming class start?

_____

Write the answer next to the letter "A"

A: ___ **1.** Peter ___ a swimming class ___ the gym today.

a. has, at   b. have, in   c. has, on   d. have, at

A: ___ **2.** Peter thought the towel was in the ___.

a. science lab   b. nurse's office   c. classroom   d. art room

A: ___ **3.** Mary saw a blue and yellow towel in the ___.

a. science lab   b. nurse's office   c. classroom   d. art room

A: ___ **4.** The art room is ___ the nurse's office.

a. across for   b. across   c. across of   d. across from

A: ___ **5.** Does Peter take any art classes now?

a. Yes, he does.   b. No, he doesn't.   c. Yes, he did.   d. No, he didn't.

A: ___ **6.** Did Peter look for his towel at Mr. Miller's office?

a. Yes, he does.   b. No, he doesn't.   c. Yes, he did.   d. No, he didn't.

A: ___ **7.** Peter's class is ___ ten minutes.

a. at   b. on   c. in   d. of

A: ___ **8.** There ___ two offices at the school.

a. was   b. are   c. were   d. is

Answers on page 373

Lesson 22: School subjects

школьные предметы

What class do you have after math?

I have an art class after math.

Learn the words

1. **science**
   естественные науки
2. **English**
   английский язык
3. **P.E.**
   физкультура
4. **geography**
   география
5. **social studies**
   социология

6. **math**
   математика
7. **art**
   изобразительное искусство
8. **music**
   музыка
9. **history**
   история
10. **computer**
    компьютер

Learn a verb

do – doing – did – done делать

Kevin: That surprises me. You always do well on science tests.

Learn an idiom

Cut class

Meaning: To miss class on purpose.

"Jenny *cut class* after she realized she didn't do her math homework."

Jessica: Hey, Kevin. Did you study for today's math test?

Kevin: Yes, but only a little. I studied more for the English test.

Jessica: Why? Your English is really good.

Kevin: I'm worried about the words. They are difficult to spell.

Jessica: I'm nervous about the science test tomorrow.

Kevin: That surprises me. You always do well on science tests.

Jessica: This semester, I cut a lot of classes.

Kevin: I'm so happy there is no history test this semester!

Jessica: Me, too. However, there was a lot of homework.

Kevin: I know. The teacher always gives a lot of history homework.

Jessica: I thought yesterday's geography test was easy.

Kevin: Really? I thought it was difficult.

Jessica: Why did you think the test was difficult?

Kevin: There were too many questions about countries in Asia.

Jessica: I traveled around Asia last year, so it was easy for me.

Kevin: You are lucky. I had no idea where half the cities were!

Jessica: Hey, what time is it now?

Kevin: It's a quarter to one.

Jessica: I better go. I have a social studies class at one o'clock.

Kevin: What class do you have after social studies?

Jessica: I have an art class after social studies.

Kevin: Me, too. I'll see you in class.

Jessica: Sure. Good luck on the English test today!

Unscramble the sentences

1. test / nervous / tomorrow / science / the / I'm / about

_____

2. yesterday's / was / I / geography / easy / thought / test

_____

3. social studies / class / an / after / have / art / I

_____

Answer the questions

1. Which test did Kevin study more for?

_____

2. Why is Jessica nervous about the science test this semester?

_____

3. Which test did they both have yesterday?

_____

4. When did Jessica travel around Asia?

_____

5. What time does the social studies class start?

_____

Write the answer next to the letter "A"

A: ___ **1.** Kevin studied ___ the English test.

a. more of   b. less for   c. more for   d. more than

A: ___ **2.** Kevin is ___ about his English test.

a. sad   b. happy   c. excited   d. worried

A: ___ **3.** Jessica always does ___ science tests.

a. badly on   b. well on   c. good for   d. bad for

A: ___ **4.** Is there a history test this semester?

a. No, it isn't.   b. No, it doesn't.   c. No, there isn't.   d. No, there doesn't.

A: ___ **5.** Jessica thought the ___ test ___ easy.

a. art, is   b. English, will be   c. geography, was   d. history, was

A: ___ **6.** Jessica ___ around Asia last year.

a. traveled   b. travels   c. travel   d. traveling

A: ___ **7.** Jessica has a social studies class ___ one o'clock.

a. in   b. at   c. on   d. by

A: ___ **8.** Which class will Jessica and Kevin have together today?

a. Art class.   b. Social studies.   c. Science.   d. Geography.

Answers on page 373

Lesson 23: Chores

работа по дому

What do you need to do today?

I need to feed the pets.

Learn the words

1. **wash the dishes**
   помыть посуду
2. **feed the pets**
   покормить животных
3. **vacuum the carpet**
   почистить пылесосом ковер
4. **take out the trash**
   вынести мусор
5. **clean the bedroom**
   сделать уборку в спальне

6. **mop the floor**
   вытереть пол
7. **cook dinner**
   приготовить ужин
8. **do the laundry**
   постирать одежду
9. **iron the clothes**
   погладить одежду
10. **make the beds**
    заправить постель

Learn a verb

know – knowing – knew – known знать

Matthew: I didn't know you can cook.

Learn an idiom

All in a day's work

Meaning: A normal day without a change in routine.

"Taking out the trash before school is *all in a day's work*."

Conversation

Matthew: Hi, Susan. How are you?

Susan: I'm a little tired. I've been doing chores all weekend.

Matthew: Is nobody helping you?

Susan: My mom is sick in bed and Dad's out working.

Matthew: What chores did you have to do?

Susan: I had to cook dinner and wash the dishes last night.

Matthew: I didn't know you can cook.

Susan: I'm not very good, but I know how to cook spaghetti.

Matthew: This morning, I fed the pets. That's an easy chore.

Susan: This morning, I vacuumed the carpet and made the beds.

Matthew: You really are busy! What do you need to do today?

Susan: I need to iron the clothes and mop the floor.

Matthew: You will be really tired later!

Susan: It's all in a day's work for my parents. I'm happy to help.

Matthew: That's very good of you.

Susan: My parents usually do all the chores every day.

Matthew: Mine, too. They're both really busy people.

Susan: I didn't realize how much there is to do around the house.

Matthew: Maybe we should both help out more.

Susan: Do you have any more chores to do this weekend?

Matthew: Yes, I do. I still have to take out the trash.

Susan: I better get back to it. I want to finish the chores and rest.

Matthew: Sounds good. Don't work too hard.

Find the mistakes and write the sentence correctly

Susan: My dad is sick in bed and Mom's out working.

_____

Susan: I need to do the laundry and make the beds.

_____

Matthew: I will be really happy later!

_____

Answer the questions

1. How is Susan feeling right now?

_____

2. Why does Susan have to do all the chores?

_____

3. Which chore did Matthew do this morning?

_____

4. What did Susan cook for dinner last night?

_____

5. Which chores does Susan still need to do today?

_____

Write the answer next to the letter "A"

A: ___ **1.** Susan has been ___ chores all day.

a. do   b. doing   c. done   d. did

A: ___ **2.** "I ___ cook dinner and wash the dishes last night."

a. had   b. have to   c. had to   d. has to

A: ___ **3.** "I ___ know you can cook."

a. don't   b. didn't   c. doesn't   d. won't

A: ___ **4.** Susan ___ how to cook spaghetti.

a. knowing   b. know   c. knew   d. knows

A: ___ **5.** Which chore didn't Susan complete?

a. Mop the floor.   b. Cook dinner.   c. Make the beds.   d. Wash the dishes.

A: ___ **6.** Which chore does Susan still need to do?

a. Wash the dishes.   b. Make the beds.   c. Cook dinner.   d. Iron the clothes.

A: ___ **7.** "It's all in a day's ___ for my parents."

a. work   b. job   c. housework   d. chore

A: ___ **8.** "___ you have any more chores to ___ this weekend?"

a. Did, did   b. Do, do   c. Does, does   d. Does, do

Answers on page 373

Lesson 24: At the toy store

в магазине игрушек

> What are you playing with?
>
> I'm playing with my ball.

Learn the words

1. **doll**
   кукла
2. **teddy bear**
   игрушечный медведь
3. **car**
   автомобиль
4. **airplane**
   самолет
5. **dinosaur**
   динозавр

6. **robot**
   робот
7. **ball**
   мяч
8. **jump rope**
   скакалка
9. **board game**
   настольная игра
10. **blocks**
    кубики

Learn a verb

borrow – borrowing – borrowed – borrowed одалживать

Dad: She'd like that. She always borrows Matthew's jump rope.

Learn an idiom

Like a kid with a new toy

Meaning: To be really happy with something.

"He was *like a kid with a new toy* when he drove the car for the first time."

Mom: We should get a gift for Susan.

Dad: That's a good idea. She really helped us a lot last week.

Mom: I know. Doing all those chores is not easy.

Dad: What do you think we should get her?

Mom: I'm not sure. What is she playing with now?

Dad: She is playing with her dolls.

Mom: We can't get her another doll. She has too many!

Dad: Susan really likes dinosaurs.

Mom: They are studying them in history class at school now.

Dad: Perhaps we can give her a book on dinosaurs.

Mom: That's an excellent idea. She'll be like a kid with a new toy.

Dad: But Susan's always inside. I'd like her to do more exercise.

Mom: I agree. Maybe we can get her a jump rope as well.

Dad: She'd like that. She always borrows Matthew's jump rope.

Mom: Let's go to the toy store and see if they have one.

Dad: Look! There is the robot from the movie we saw last week.

Mom: I don't think Susan would like a robot.

Dad: It would look great on my desk in the office.

Mom: You're like a little boy!

Dad: Can I get the robot?

Mom: Yes, but let's find a jump rope for Susan first.

Dad: Here's a green one. That's Susan's favorite color.

Mom: Since you're getting the robot, I'm getting this board game!

Put the sentences in order

Mom: I know. Doing all those chores is not easy. ___

Dad: What do you think we should get her? ___

Mom: I'm not sure. What is she playing with now? ___

Dad: That's a good idea. She really helped us a lot last week. ___

Mom: We should get a gift for Susan. ___

Dad: Susan really likes dinosaurs. ___

Mom: We can't get her another doll. She has too many! ___

Dad: She is playing with her dolls. ___

Answer the questions

1. What did Susan help her parents do last week?

_____

2. Why didn't Mom want to get Susan another doll?

_____

3. What is Susan learning about in history class?

_____

4. Where does Dad want to put the robot?

_____

5. What does Mom want to buy for herself?

_____

Write the answer next to the letter "A"

A: ___ **1.** "We should get a gift ___ Susan."

a. give   b. to   c. of   d. for

A: ___ **2.** "___ all the chores ___ not easy."

a. Do, is   b. Doing, is   c. Done, are   d. Doing, are

A: ___ **3.** Will Susan's parents get her a doll?

a. Yes, they will.   b. No, they won't.   c. Yes, they did.   d. No, they don't.

A: ___ **4.** What did Susan's father suggest to get a book about?

a. Dinosaurs.   b. Dolls.   c. Jump ropes.   d. Robots.

A: ___ **5.** There ___ a robot at the toy store from the movie they had seen.

a. has   b. were   c. was   d. have

A: ___ **6.** Where ___ Susan's father ___ to go?

a. does, wants   b. do, want   c. did, wanted   d. does, want

A: ___ **7.** Susan's mother ___ Susan would like a robot.

a. isn't thinking   b. didn't thought   c. doesn't think   d. don't think

A: ___ **8.** Mom wanted to find a ___ before getting the ___.

a. jump rope, robot   b. robot, jump rope   c. doll, robot   d. board game, doll

Answers on page 373

Lesson 25: In the kitchen

в кухне

What was he cleaning?

He was cleaning the stove.

Learn the words

1. **refrigerator**
   холодильник
2. **coffee maker**
   кофеварка
3. **microwave oven**
   микроволновая печь
4. **stove**
   плита
5. **blender**
   блендер

6. **cupboard**
   кухонный шкаф
7. **rice cooker**
   рисоварка
8. **dish rack**
   сушилка для посуды
9. **pan**
   сковорода
10. **toaster**
    тостер

Learn a verb

clean – cleaning – cleaned – cleaned чистить, убирать

Kevin: Mom asked me to clean the things in the kitchen.

Learn an idiom

Too many cooks in the kitchen

Meaning: When too many people try to take control.

"We couldn't find a solution because there were *too many cooks in the kitchen*."

Peter: We haven't spoken for a while, so I thought I'd phone you.

Kevin: Sorry, I've been really busy lately.

Peter: What have you been doing?

Kevin: Recently, I spoke to Susan about doing more chores.

Peter: Why do you want to do more chores?

Kevin: I think it's good to help Mom and Dad.

Peter: What chores have you been doing?

Kevin: Mom asked me to clean the things in the kitchen.

Peter: I see. What were you cleaning?

Kevin: I was cleaning the stove and cupboard yesterday.

Peter: What else were you cleaning?

Kevin: This morning, I was cleaning the refrigerator.

Peter: Cleaning the refrigerator is not easy.

Kevin: I know. You have to take everything out first.

Peter: Mom has been replacing a few old items in our kitchen.

Kevin: What did she replace?

Peter: She replaced the toaster and rice cooker. They're too old.

Kevin: I hope she didn't replace the blender. It's the best!

Peter: Of course not! I would be so upset.

Kevin: How about the coffee maker?

Peter: Yes, that's also gone, but Mom hasn't bought a new one yet.

Kevin: I bet your dad wasn't happy. Did he say anything to her?

Peter: Mom told him that there are too many cooks in the kitchen!

Fill in the blanks

Kevin: Recently, I _____ to Susan about doing _____ chores.

Peter: Mom has been _____ a few old items in our _____.

Peter: _____ the refrigerator is not _____.

Kevin: Mom _____ me to clean the _____ in the kitchen.

Kevin: I hope she _____ replace the _____. It's the _____!

Peter: Of _____ not! I _____ be so upset.

Kevin: I bet your dad _____ happy. Did he say _____ to her?

Answer the questions

1. Who did Kevin speak to about doing chores?

_____

2. Why does Kevin want to do more chores?

_____

3. What was Kevin cleaning yesterday?

_____

4. What has Peter's mother been doing in the kitchen?

_____

5. Why did Peter's mother want to replace the toaster?

_____

Write the answer next to the letter "A"

A: ___ **1.** Were Kevin and Peter talking on the phone?

a. No, they weren't.   b. No, they wasn't.   c. Yes, they was.   d. Yes, they were.

A: ___ **2.** Kevin spoke to Susan about ___ more chores.

a. do   b. doing   c. did   d. done

A: ___ **3.** Kevin ___ it's good ___ help his parents.

a. thinks, to   b. think, of   c. thinks, for   d. think, to

A: ___ **4.** Kevin was ___ the stove and cupboard yesterday.

a. cleaned   b. cleaning   c. clean   d. cleans

A: ___ **5.** Peter thinks cleaning the ___ is not easy.

a. stove   b. toaster   c. blender   d. refrigerator

A: ___ **6.** What ___ Peter's mother been doing?

a. had   b. was   c. has   d. is

A: ___ **7.** Has Peter's mother bought a new coffee maker yet?

a. No, she didn't.   b. Yes, she did.   c. No, she hasn't.   d. Yes, she has.

A: ___ **8.** Peter's father really likes the ___.

a. coffee maker   b. toaster   c. blender   d. rice cooker

Answers on page 373

Lesson 26: In the toolbox

в ящике для инструментов

What were you using to fix the chair?
I was using the electric drill.

Learn the words

1. hammer
молоток

2. electric drill
электродрель

3. screwdriver
отвертка

4. paintbrush
кисть

5. shovel
лопата

6. tape measure
рулетка

7. axe
топор

8. pliers
плоскогубцы

9. ladder
стремянка

10. wrench
ключ

Learn a verb

use – using – used – used использовать

Dad: You can check. Use the tape measure to measure the size.

Learn an idiom

Tools of the trade

Meaning: Things that are needed for a specific job.

"My cell phone, diary and calculator are all *tools of the trade*."

Dad: Peter, Mom asked me to fix the cupboard in the kitchen.

Peter: What's wrong with the cupboard?

Dad: The cupboard door doesn't close properly.

Peter: Do you need my help?

Dad: Yes, please. Hand me the tools while I'm up on the ladder.

Peter: Sure. Which tool do you need?

Dad: We need to unscrew the door first. Hand me a screwdriver.

Peter: I can't find it. It's not in the toolbox.

Dad: It should be there. I was using it to fix the chair yesterday.

Peter: Oh, here it is. It was under the wrench.

Dad: Forget the screwdriver. I'll use the electric drill instead.

Peter: Why do you want to use an electric drill?

Dad: The screws are old and difficult to turn.

Peter: Maybe you should use a hammer!

Dad: Let's stick to the tools of the trade. The electric drill, please.

Peter: Good job! But you've scratched the cupboard.

Dad: That's okay. I'll paint over the scratch.

Peter: Here's the paintbrush. What color paint do you need?

Dad: We'll keep the color the same. Give me the white paint.

Peter: Do we need to replace the cupboard door?

Dad: You can check. Use the tape measure to measure the size.

Peter: The measurements are the right size.

Dad: That's good news. The problem must be the old screws then.

Unscramble the sentences

1. door / cupboard / The / close / properly / doesn't

_____

2. old / turn / are / The / and / to / screws / difficult

_____

3. right / The / size / the / are / measurements

_____

Answer the questions

1. What does Peter's mother want his father to fix?

_____

2. Who was standing up on the ladder?

_____

3. What was the first tool that Peter gave his father?

_____

4. Why did Dad want to use the electric drill?

_____

5. Which tool did Peter use to measure the cupboard door?

_____

Write the answer next to the letter "A"

A: ___ **1.** "The cupboard door ___ close ___."

a. won't, good   b. didn't, proper   c. don't, proper   d. doesn't, properly

A: ___ **2.** "___ you need my help?"

a. Have   b. Does   c. Do   d. Are

A: ___ **3.** The screwdriver was ___ the ___.

a. by, paintbrush   b. under, wrench   c. on, hammer   d. under, ladder

A: ___ **4.** Did they change the color of the cupboard door?

a. Yes, they did.   b. No, they didn't.   c. No, they don't.   d. Yes, they do.

A: ___ **5.** What did Dad use to fix the chair? He used a ___.

a. pliers   b. screwdriver   c. hammer   d. shovel

A: ___ **6.** Which tool did they not use to fix the cupboard?

a. Screwdriver.   b. Ladder.   c. Pliers.   d. Tape measure.

A: ___ **7.** Did they replace the cupboard door?

a. No, they didn't.   b. Yes, they did.   c. No, they hadn't.   d. Yes, they had.

A: ___ **8.** Peter said the measurement of the cupboard door was ___.

a. wrong   b. right   c. bad   d. correctly

Answers on page 373

Lesson 27: Transportation

транспорт

How will you be going to Rome?

I will be taking a bus.

Learn the words

1. catch a bus
сесть на автобус

2. take a taxi
взять такси

3. take a ferry
сесть на паром

4. ride a motorcycle
водить мотоцикл

5. take the subway
поехать на метро

6. take a train
сесть на поезд

7. drive a car
водить машину

8. ride a scooter
водить скутер

9. ride a bicycle
ехать на велосипеде

10. take an airplane
полететь на самолете

Learn a verb

take – taking – took – taken брать

Emily: After Sydney, I'll be taking a train to Melbourne.

Learn an idiom

Lose one's train of thought

Meaning: To forget what you were thinking about.

"I'm sorry, I *lost my train of thought*. What were we talking about?"

Helen: Are you going anywhere this summer?

Emily: Yes, I am. I'm going to Sydney.

Helen: Great! How will you be going to Sydney?

Emily: I'll be taking an airplane.

Helen: That sounds great. Will you go anywhere else?

Emily: After Sydney, I'll be taking a train to Melbourne.

Helen: Why do you want to go to Melbourne?

Emily: I would like to see the penguins.

Helen: Will you be going to the zoo?

Emily: No, I won't be. You can see penguins on a nearby island.

Helen: I didn't know that you can see penguins in Australia.

Emily: Yes, you can. We'll be taking a ferry to the island.

Helen: Your summer sounds better than mine.

Emily: Why? What will you be doing?

Helen: I'll be staying at my grandparent's house on the farm.

Emily: That doesn't sound too bad.

Helen: True. At least I won't be taking the subway every day.

Emily: What will you do on the farm?

Helen: I'm sorry. I lost my train of thought. What did you ask?

Emily: What will you be doing while you're staying on the farm?

Helen: My brother and I love to ride motorcycles over the hills.

Emily: That sounds really fun! I've only ever ridden a bicycle.

Helen: Yes, you're right. We will both have a great summer!

Find the mistakes and write the sentence correctly

Emily: Before Sydney, I'll be taking a bus to Melbourne.

_____

Helen: My summer sounds better than yours.

_____

Helen: My sister and I love to ride bicycles over the hills.

_____

Answer the questions

1. Where is Emily going this summer?

_____

2. How will Emily be going to Melbourne?

_____

3. Why does Emily want to go to Melbourne?

_____

4. Where is Helen going this summer?

_____

5. What will Helen be doing with her brother?

_____

Write the answer next to the letter "A"

A: ___ **1.** Emily will ___ to Sydney this summer.

a. going   b. be going   c. be go   d. have go

A: ___ **2.** Emily will be ___ an airplane to Sydney.

a. driving   b. catching   c. riding   d. taking

A: ___ **3.** Emily ___ to see the penguins.

a. would   b. like   c. want   d. would like

A: ___ **4.** Helen didn't know there ___ penguins in Australia.

a. have   b. are   c. is   d. was

A: ___ **5.** Emily will be taking a ___ to the island.

a. ferry   b. bus   c. train   d. subway

A: ___ **6.** Will Helen be going to Sydney with Emily?

a. No, she will.   b. No, she will not.   c. No, she won't be.   d. No, she won't.

A: ___ **7.** Helen lost her train ___ thought.

a. in   b. with   c. of   d. for

A: ___ **8.** Emily ___ only ever ___ a bicycle.

a. has, ridden   b. has, ride   c. have, rode   d. have, ridden

Answers on page 373

Lesson 28: Clothes

одежда

Whose jacket is that?

It's mine.

Learn the words

1. T-shirt
футболка

2. blouse
блузка

3. scarf
шарф

4. coat
пальто

5. dress
платье

6. hat
шапка

7. sweater
свитер

8. jacket
куртка, пиджак

9. skirt
юбка

10. necktie
галстук

Learn a verb

wear – wearing – wore – worn носить

Susan: Right now, I'm wearing a skirt. I think I should change.

Learn an idiom

Wear somebody out

Meaning: To make someone tired.

"My boss completely *wore me out* today."

Conversation

Jessica: Are you ready to go?

Susan: Not yet. I don't know what to wear.

Jessica: We're going hiking, so you don't need a pretty dress!

Susan: Are you sure we can go hiking today? It's pretty cold.

Jessica: I checked the weather. It's not going to rain.

Susan: Right now, I'm wearing a skirt. I think I should change.

Jessica: Yes, you should. I suggest you wear a pair of pants.

Susan: I like the jacket you're wearing. Whose jacket is that?

Jessica: It's my sister's jacket. She's lending it to me for a day.

Susan: I only have this purple coat.

Jessica: Perhaps you should also wear a sweater underneath.

Susan: That's a good idea. I have a sweater in my bag.

Jessica: I'm only wearing a T-shirt, but this jacket is really warm.

Susan: Okay, I think I'm ready to go.

Jessica: I've prepared two water bottles and some fruit.

Susan: Thanks. I heard the mountain we're hiking is really high.

Jessica: It is. We are definitely going to be worn out.

Susan: I agree. We can take a rest at the top of the mountain.

Jessica: The view from the top should be really beautiful.

Susan: I'm worried that it will be too cloudy.

Jessica: I think you're right. I'm not going to bring my hat.

Susan: Me, neither. It's not a sunny day today.

Jessica: I think we've got everything we need. Let's go hiking!

Put the sentences in order

Susan: Not yet. I don't know what to wear. ____

Jessica: I checked the weather. It's not going to rain. ____

Susan: I like the jacket you're wearing. Whose jacket is that? ____

Jessica: We're going hiking, so you don't need a pretty dress! ____

Susan: Are you sure we can go hiking today? It's pretty cold. ____

Jessica: Are you ready to go? ____

Susan: Right now, I'm wearing a skirt. I think I should change. ____

Jessica: Yes, you should. I suggest you wear a pair of pants. ____

Answer the questions

1. Who doesn't know what to wear?

_____

2. What did Jessica suggest to wear?

_____

3. What does Susan have in her bag?

_____

4. How many bottles did Jessica prepare?

_____

5. Why aren't they bringing a hat?

_____

Write the answer next to the letter "A"

A: ___ **1.** Susan ___ know what to wear.

a. not   b. isn't   c. doesn't   d. don't

A: ___ **2.** Susan is concerned about the weather ___ too cold to go hiking.

a. be   b. being   c. is   d. was

A: ___ **3.** Susan is ___ a skirt.

a. wear   b. wore   c. wearing   d. wears

A: ___ **4.** "I suggest you wear ___ pants."

a. pair of   b. pairs of   c. a pair   d. a pair of

A: ___ **5.** "I've prepared two water ___ and ___ fruit."

a. bottle, some   b. bottles, any   c. bottle, a lot of   d. bottles, some

A: ___ **6.** "I heard the mountain we're hiking ___ high."

a. really   b. real   c. is really   d. is real

A: ___ **7.** ___ Susan have a sweater in her bag? Yes, she ___.

a. Does, does   b. Does, did   c. Do, does   d. Do, do

A: ___ **8.** Susan ___ that the weather will be too cloudy.

a. is worry   b. is worried   c. worry   d. worried

Answers on page 373

Lesson 29: More clothes

ещё одежда

Whose jeans are these?

They're mine.

Learn the words

1. pants
брюки

2. shorts
шорты

3. shoes
туфли, ботинки

4. dresses
платья

5. shirts
рубашки

6. jeans
джинсы

7. socks
носки

8. gloves
перчатки

9. pajamas
пижамы

10. boots
сапоги

Learn a verb

lend – lending – lent – lent давать в долг

John: These shoes are my brother's. He lent them to me.

Learn an idiom

Fits like a glove

Meaning: Something is the right size.

"The new shirt you bought me *fits like a glove*."

Matthew: Thanks for coming with me to the clothes store.

John: You're welcome. I'm happy to help.

Matthew: Mom said I need to buy some clothes for summer.

John: I need to buy some shoes. My shoes are getting old.

Matthew: Your shoes don't look old. Whose shoes are those?

John: These shoes are my brother's. He lent them to me.

Matthew: Maybe we can go to the shoe shop later.

John: That would be great. So, what do you need for summer?

Matthew: I think it's too hot to wear jeans, so I'd like some shorts.

John: I read that this year will be the hottest summer.

Matthew: I better get some shirts, too.

John: There are summer pants you can also buy.

Matthew: What are summer pants?

John: They are lightweight pants made of cotton.

Matthew: I can wear them when I work. They fit like a glove, too.

John: Do you have a job now?

Matthew: Yes, I'm working at the Thai restaurant as a waiter.

John: That's great! How long have you been working there?

Matthew: I've been working there since last Monday.

John: I think the clothes you chose look great.

Matthew: Me, too. Let's go to the shoe shop now.

John: The shoe shop sells sports socks as well.

Matthew: All my socks have holes in them, so get me ten pairs!

Fill in the blanks

Matthew: Mom said I need to buy some _____ for _____.

John: These shoes are my _____. He _____ them to me.

Matthew: _____ we can go to the shoe shop _____.

John: They are _____ pants made of _____.

Matthew: Yes, I'm _____ at the Thai _____ as a waiter.

Matthew: I've _____ working there _____ last Monday.

John: The shoe shop _____ sports socks as _____.

Answer the questions

1. Where are the boys?

_____

2. Is John wearing his brother's shoes?

_____

3. Where is Matthew working now?

_____

4. When did Matthew start working at the Thai restaurant?

_____

5. What does John need to buy?

_____

Write the answer next to the letter "A"

A: ___ **1.** "Thanks ___ coming ___ me to the clothes store."

a. for, to   b. of, with   c. to, for   d. for, with

A: ___ **2.** John ___ some new shoes because his ___ getting old.

a. need, is   b. needs, are   c. needed, was   d. wants, is

A: ___ **3.** John's brother ___ a pair of shoes to him.

a. lend   b. lent   c. borrowed   d. lending

A: ___ **4.** Matthew thinks it's too hot to wear ___, so he wants to buy ___.

a. jeans, shorts   b. shorts, jeans   c. pants, shorts   d. shorts, pants

A: ___ **5.** John read that this year will be ___ summer.

a. the hotter   b. the hot   c. the hottest   d. hottest

A: ___ **6.** The lightweight pants ___ cotton.

a. made from   b. are made of   c. are made for   d. is made of

A: ___ **7.** Matthew is working at a Thai restaurant ___ a waiter.

a. as   b. be   c. to be   d. is

A: ___ **8.** Which clothes did the two boys not talk about?

a. Shorts.   b. Pajamas.   c. Jeans.   d. Pants.

Answers on page 373

Lesson 30: In the living room

в гостиной

Where is the coffee table?

It's in front of the sofa.

Learn the words

1. **bookcase**
   книжный шкаф
2. **television**
   телевизор
3. **clock**
   часы
4. **coffee table**
   кофейный столик
5. **armchair**
   кресло

6. **painting**
   картина
7. **TV stand**
   тумба для телевизора
8. **rug**
   ковер
9. **sofa**
   диван
10. **vase**
    ваза

Learn a verb

move – moving – moved – moved двигаться

Eric: The sofa is the biggest thing, so let's move that first.

Learn an idiom

A race against the clock

Meaning: To not have too much time left to complete a task.

"It's *a race against the clock* to finish this project."

Betty: Thanks for helping me move into my new apartment.

Eric: It's no problem. However, I only have one hour to help.

Betty: Let's start with the living room furniture then.

Eric: Good idea. The furniture is the most difficult to move.

Betty: I have a lot of stuff, so it's a race against the clock!

Eric: The sofa is the biggest thing, so let's move that first.

Betty: Put the sofa against the wall.

Eric: This sofa is too heavy for me. You need to take one end.

Betty: Sure. It'll be easier to move with two people.

Eric: Okay, so what's the next thing to move?

Betty: Please put the big vase on the left of the sofa.

Eric: That looks good, but you need a nice plant to put in the vase.

Betty: My aunt said she'd give me one as a housewarming gift.

Eric: Do you want the coffee table in the middle of the living room?

Betty: Yes, but first put a rug on the floor.

Eric: Should the rug go underneath the coffee table?

Betty: Yes, it should. I don't want the table to scratch the floor.

Eric: I guess the TV stand should be across from the sofa?

Betty: That's right. And move the bookcase next to the TV stand.

Eric: I've plugged the television in, so it's ready to use.

Betty: The clock can go in my bedroom. Just leave it on the sofa.

Eric: This painting is beautiful. I love it!

Betty: Eric, you've been such a great help today. You can have it.

Unscramble the sentences

1. left / put / sofa / the / vase / the / of / Please / the / on / big

_____

2. the / to / don't / floor / scratch / table / I / the / want

_____

3. to / furniture / the / is / move / difficult / The / most

_____

Answer the questions

1. How long can Eric help Betty?

_____

2. What will they move to the living room first?

_____

3. Could Eric move the sofa by himself?

_____

4. What was put next to the TV stand?

_____

5. What did Betty give Eric for helping her?

_____

Write the answer next to the letter "A"

A: ___ **1.** "Thanks ___ helping me ___ into my new apartment."

a. for, moves   b. to, move   c. to, moving   d. for, move

A: ___ **2.** Eric only ___ one hour to help Betty.

a. got   b. has   c. have   d. is

A: ___ **3.** The furniture is ___ difficult to move.

a. the more   b. more   c. the most   d. most

A: ___ **4.** "I have a lot of stuff, ___ it's a race ___ the clock!"

a. so, against   b. but, for   c. so, on   d. but, to

A: ___ **5.** Will Betty's uncle give her a plant? No, her aunt ___.

a. does   b. will be   c. did   d. will

A: ___ **6.** The ___ is next to the TV stand.

a. sofa   b. bookcase   c. television   d. coffee table

A: ___ **7.** Which item did Eric not help Betty move?

a. Sofa.   b. Armchair.   c. Coffee table.   d. Bookcase.

A: ___ **8.** Betty put the rug ___ the coffee table.

a. on   b. by   c. underneath   d. below

Answers on page 373

Lesson 31: In the bathroom

в ванной комнате

What is above the sink?

There is a mirror above the sink.

Learn the words

1. mirror
зеркало

2. bath towel
банное полотенце

3. shower
душ

4. toilet paper
туалетная бумага

5. bath mat
коврик для ванной

6. shelf
полка

7. sink
мойка

8. toilet
унитаз

9. bathtub
ванна

10. soap
мыло

Learn a verb

wash – washing – washed – washed мыть

Emily: No, there isn't. We still haven't washed everything.

Learn an idiom

Throw in the towel

Meaning: To give up or quit.

"After trying three times, he decided to *throw in the towel*."

Bob: Hey, I heard you were fixing your bathroom.

Emily: Yes, we decided to change some things and improve it.

Bob: When did you do all this work?

Emily: I had some time last month, so I worked on weekends.

Bob: Did you do the work all by yourself?

Emily: My aunt helped me. I borrowed some tools from my uncle.

Bob: What kinds of things did you change?

Emily: Well, we bought a new toilet, bathtub, and bath mat.

Bob: Wow! That really sounds like a lot of hard work!

Emily: Yeah, a few times I wanted to throw in the towel.

Bob: You did a lot. So, what is beside the sink now?

Emily: There is a shelf beside the sink. I use it to put the soap on.

Bob: Is there a mirror above the sink?

Emily: No, there isn't. There is a large mirror next to the shower.

Bob: What is beside the bathtub?

Emily: There is a new bath mat beside the bathtub.

Bob: Where do you put your bath towels?

Emily: After we wash them, there is a shelf beside the shower.

Bob: So there are towels on the shelf now?

Emily: No, there aren't any bath towels in the bathroom.

Bob: It isn't finished yet? Is there toilet paper beside the toilet?

Emily: No, there isn't. We still haven't washed everything.

Bob: I have to go home then. I need to use a bathroom!

Find the mistakes and write the sentence correctly

Emily: I had some time last week, so she worked on Mondays.

_____

Emily: No, it isn't. There is a small mirror next to the toilet.

_____

Emily: There is an old bath mat across from the shower.

_____

Answer the questions

1. When did Emily do all the work?

_____

2. Who did Emily borrow some tools from?

_____

3. Where does Emily put the soap?

_____

4. What is beside the bathtub?

_____

5. Why does Bob need to go home?

_____

Write the answer next to the letter "A"

A: ___ **1.** Emily ___ her bathroom last ___.

a. fixed, month   b. washed, month   c. changed, week   d. fix, weekend

A: ___ **2.** Emily's uncle ___ her some tools.

a. borrowed   b. bought   c. sold   d. lent

A: ___ **3.** Sometimes she felt like she wanted to throw in the ___.

a. toilet   b. bathtub   c. soap   d. towel

A: ___ **4.** Is there a shelf below the sink?

a. Yes, there is.   b. No, there isn't.   c. Yes, it is.   d. No, there hasn't.

A: ___ **5.** There is a ___ next to the shower.

a. soap   b. sink   c. mirror   d. bath mat

A: ___ **6.** Emily bought a new ___ and ___.

a. bathtub, shelf   b. toilet, soap   c. bathtub, toilet   d. bath mat, sink

A: ___ **7.** Emily still hasn't ___ everything.

a. fixed   b. washed   c. bought   d. borrowed

A: ___ **8.** Are there any bath towels in the bathroom?

a. Yes, there are.   b. Yes, they have.   c. No, there aren't.   d. No, they haven't.

Answers on page 373

Lesson 32: In the bedroom

в спальне

Learn the words

1. **bed**
   кровать
2. **pillow**
   подушка
3. **mattress**
   матрас
4. **blanket**
   одеяло
5. **drawers**
   комод

6. **lamp**
   лампа
7. **alarm clock**
   будильник
8. **wardrobe**
   гардероб
9. **bed sheets**
   простыня
10. **nightstand**
   прикроватная тумба

Learn a verb

change – changing – changed – changed менять, меняться

Jack: Yes, I want to change my mattress and pillow, too.

Learn an idiom

Get up on the wrong side of the bed

Meaning: To describe somebody who is in a bad mood.

"Mom's in a really bad mood. I think she *got up on the wrong side of the bed*."

Amy: I heard you moved into a new house.

Jack: That's right, but I still have to get a few more things.

Amy: What do you need to get?

Jack: For example, there aren't any drawers on the left of the bed.

Amy: Is there a nightstand on the left of the bed?

Jack: Yes, there is. I put my alarm clock and lamp on it.

Amy: I see. What is on the right of the bed?

Jack: There is a wardrobe on the right of the bed.

Amy: Do you need to get anything else for your new room?

Jack: Yes, I want to change my mattress and pillow, too.

Amy: You really need to get a lot for your bedroom.

Jack: Yes. It's a nice room, but it's a bit empty right now.

Amy: That's great! We should go to the mall together.

Jack: Do you want to go shopping for your bedroom, too?

Amy: Yes, I need to buy some new bed sheets and a blanket.

Jack: Yeah, now that it's December it's really cold at night.

Amy: Let's ask Kevin to go with us, I think he needs a new lamp.

Jack: I talked to him this morning, but he wasn't in a good mood.

Amy: Why was he so unhappy?

Jack: I guess he just got up on the wrong side of the bed.

Amy: Well, I'm sure that buying new stuff would change his mood.

Jack: Why do you think that?

Amy: Every time I have a bad mood, shopping makes me happy.

Put the sentences in order

Jack: Yes. It's a nice room but it's a bit empty right now. ____

Amy: Yes, I need to buy some new bed sheets and a blanket. ____

Amy: Do you need to get anything else for your new room? ____

Amy: That's great! We should go to the mall together. ____

Jack: Yeah, now that it's December it's really cold at night. ____

Jack: Yes, I want to change my mattress and pillow, too. ____

Jack: Do you want to go shopping for your bedroom, too? ____

Amy: You really need to get a lot for your bedroom. ____

Answer the questions

1. Where is Jack's nightstand?

_____

2. What is on the right of the bed?

_____

3. Where does Amy want to go?

_____

4. Who needs a new lamp?

_____

5. When did Jack talk to Kevin?

_____

Write the answer next to the letter "A"

A: ___ **1.** Jack still ___ to get a few more things.

a. have   b. must   c. need   d. has

A: ___ **2.** Are there any drawers on the left of the bed?

a. No, there aren't.   b. Yes, there is.   c. No, there isn't.   d. Yes, there are.

A: ___ **3.** Jack ___ his lamp on the nightstand.

a. keep   b. puts   c. wants   d. putting

A: ___ **4.** There is a wardrobe on the ___ of the ___.

a. left, lamp   b. left, room   c. right, bed   d. right, drawers

A: ___ **5.** Jack wants to ___ his pillow.

a. changing   b. changed   c. change   d. changes

A: ___ **6.** ___ needs to buy new bed sheets.

a. Jack   b. Amy   c. Kevin   d. December

A: ___ **7.** Their friend woke up on the ___ side of the ___.

a. wrong, bed   b. right, blanket   c. left, bed   d. left, pillow

A: ___ **8.** Shopping ___ Amy ___.

a. make, happy   b. has, unhappy   c. mall, likes   d. makes, happy

Answers on page 373

Lesson 33: Around the house

возле дома

What will he be doing this weekend?

He will be fixing the gate.

Learn the words

1. **work in the garage**
   работать в гараже
2. **fix the mailbox**
   починить почтовый ящик
3. **fix the gate**
   починить ворота
4. **work in the garden**
   работать в саду
5. **clean the pool**
   почистить бассейн

6. **work in the yard**
   работать во дворе
7. **fix the fence**
   починить забор
8. **clean the balcony**
   сделать уборку на балконе
9. **clean the outdoor furniture**
   почистить наружную мебель
10. **clean the barbecue**
    почистить гриль

Learn a verb

fix – fixing – fixed – fixed чинить

Max: Ted can't come because he'll be fixing the gate.

Learn an idiom

On the house

Meaning: To get something for free.

"The waiter apologized and gave him the meal *on the house*."

Max: This weekend the weather will be good. Let's go to the park.

Julie: That's a good idea, we can play soccer. Can Ted come?

Max: He can't come because he'll be fixing the gate. Let's ask Bob.

Julie: Bob will be cleaning the outdoor furniture this weekend.

Max: What will Susan be doing on Saturday?

Julie: She'll be working in the yard. She'll also be fixing the fence.

Max: What will Emily be doing this weekend?

Julie: She won't be working in the garden. She hurt her foot.

Max: That means she can't play soccer, too. No one can play.

Julie: Well, there are many things to do around the house, too.

Max: What do you mean? It's Friday today. I want to relax.

Julie: Mom will be cleaning the pool. Dad will be fixing the mailbox.

Max: Right. I also heard Dad will be working in the garage.

Julie: It seems like we're the only people who won't be working.

Max: Will Mom be cleaning the balcony, too? It's really dirty.

Julie: Yes, she will be. We should probably help her.

Max: I think you're right, but first we should eat something.

Julie: Yes, we can eat the hot dogs that I got for free.

Max: Why did the supermarket give you hot dogs on the house?

Julie: They were a gift because I bought so many things.

Max: We can barbecue them. Now, I'll be busy this weekend, too.

Julie: Why? What will you be doing this weekend?

Max: I'll be cleaning the barbecue tomorrow.

Fill in the blanks

Max: What _____ Susan be _____ on Saturday?

Julie: She'll be _____ in the yard. She'll be _____ the fence.

Max: _____ will Emily be doing this _____?

Julie: She _____ be _____ in the garden. She hurt her foot.

Max: That _____ she can't _____ soccer, too.

Julie: Well, _____ are many things to do _____ the house.

Max: What do you _____? It's Friday _____. I want to relax.

Answer the questions

1. Why can't Ted play soccer this weekend?

_____

2. When will Susan be working in the yard?

_____

3. Who will be cleaning the pool?

_____

4. Where did Julie get the hot dogs?

_____

5. What will Max be doing tomorrow?

_____

Write the answer next to the letter "A"

A: ___ **1.** Julie ___ to ___ soccer at the park.

a. want, plays   b. like, do   c. wants, play   d. likes, doing

A: ___ **2.** Susan will be ___ the ___.

a. fixing, gate   b. cleaning, pool   c. cleaning, balcony   d. fixing, fence

A: ___ **3.** Will Susan be working in the yard on Sunday?

a. No, she can't.   b. Yes, she can.   c. No, she won't be.   d. Yes, she will be.

A: ___ **4.** There are many things to do ___ the house.

a. on   b. around   c. through   d. working

A: ___ **5.** Mom will be ___ the pool.

a. swimming   b. cleaning   c. fixing   d. working

A: ___ **6.** The ___ is really ___.

a. balcony, dirty   b. gate, fixing   c. yard, working   d. pool, broken

A: ___ **7.** The hot dogs were ___ the house.

a. around   b. in   c. through   d. on

A: ___ **8.** Max will be cleaning the ___ this weekend.

a. barbecue   b. mailbox   c. hot dogs   d. garage

Answers on page 373

Lesson 34: Hobbies

хобби

What do you enjoy doing on the weekend?

I enjoy going hiking.

Learn the words

1. **do gardening**
   заниматься садоводством
2. **go hiking**
   ходить в поход
3. **take photographs**
   снимать фотографии
4. **play video games**
   играть в видеоигры
5. **listen to music**
   слушать музыку

6. **go camping**
   ездить в поход с ночлегом
7. **play chess**
   играть в шахматы
8. **watch movies**
   смотреть фильмы
9. **go fishing**
   ездить на рыбалку
10. **sing karaoke**
    петь караоке

Learn a verb

enjoy – enjoying – enjoyed – enjoyed получать удовольствие

Kate: I think it's a really good idea to enjoy many hobbies.

Learn an idiom

Face the music

Meaning: To face the consequences of one's actions.

"You need to own up to your mistake and *face the music*."

Kate: I just watched a really good movie at the cinema.

Peter: That sounds fun. Who did you go with?

Kate: Matthew. He enjoys watching movies every day.

Peter: Yes. He has many other hobbies, too.

Kate: Oh? What else does he enjoy doing?

Peter: He also enjoys listening to music and going hiking.

Kate: I think it's a really good idea to enjoy many hobbies.

Peter: I agree. What do you enjoy doing on the weekend?

Kate: I enjoy taking photographs and playing chess.

Peter: Do you like playing video games?

Kate: No, I enjoy doing gardening. I like to be outside.

Peter: That's probably a good idea.

Kate: I remember you like playing video games a lot.

Peter: Yeah, but now I have to face the music.

Kate: I heard your grades at school weren't very good.

Peter: Yes, so now I have to fix the problem.

Kate: You could try a new outdoor hobby.

Peter: My brother enjoys going camping and going fishing.

Kate: You and your brother could do the same hobbies together.

Peter: Thanks for the idea. I think we'll go next Saturday.

Kate: Also, do you enjoy singing karaoke?

Peter: Yes, I do. Why do you ask?

Kate: On Sunday, we'll sing karaoke. You two can come along.

Unscramble the sentences

1. has / other / too / Yes / many / he / hobbies

_____

2. playing / taking / and / enjoy / I / chess / photographs

_____

3. like / games / you / video / Do / playing

_____

Answer the questions

1. Who enjoys watching movies every day?

_____

2. What does Kate think is a good idea to enjoy?

_____

3. Does Kate like playing video games?

_____

4. Why does Peter have to face the music?

_____

5. When will Peter go camping?

_____

Write the answer next to the letter "A"

A: ___ **1.** Kate just ___ a really good movie.

a. watching   b. watched   c. watch   d. watches

A: ___ **2.** ___ has many other hobbies.

a. Kate   b. Peter   c. Kate's brother   d. Matthew

A: ___ **3.** Kate ___ enjoy ___ video games.

a. don't, play   b. doesn't, playing   c. really, playing   d. don't, playing

A: ___ **4.** Does Kate enjoy playing chess on the weekend?

a. Yes, she do. b. Yes, she enjoy.   c. No, she doesn't.   d. Yes, she does.

A: ___ **5.** Peter has bad grades, so he has to ___ the ___.

a. play, music   b. sing, karaoke   c. face, music   d. taste, problem

A: ___ **6.** Peter's brother ___ going ___.

a. enjoy, camp   b. enjoys, fish   c. enjoys, camping   d. enjoy, fishing

A: ___ **7.** Who enjoys taking photographs on the weekend?

a. Kate.   b. Matthew.   c. Peter.   d. Peter's brother.

A: ___ **8.** They will ___ karaoke on ___.

a. sing, Sunday b. singing, Sunday c. face, Sunday d. singing, Saturday

Answers on page 373

Lesson 35: Countries

страны

Which countries have you been to?

I have been to Brazil and Mexico.

Learn the words

1. Japan
Япония

2. Canada
Канада

3. Brazil
Бразилия

4. Australia
Австралия

5. South Africa
Южная Африка

6. China
Китай

7. Mexico
Мексика

8. Argentina
Аргентина

9. New Zealand
Новая Зеландия

10. Kenya
Кения

Learn a verb

write – writing – wrote – written писать

John: Yes, he wrote a book about traveling there.

Learn an idiom

Second to none

Meaning: To describe something that is the best.

"The mountains in Canada are *second to none* for skiing."

John: You look pretty tired. Didn't you sleep well?

Helen: Actually, I just got back from traveling, so I'm very sleepy.

John: Oh right! I heard you went on a trip with your sister.

Helen: Yes, we traveled to Mexico. Have you been to Mexico?

John: Yes, I have. The beaches there are second to none.

Helen: Yes, they were great. We went swimming every day.

John: I remember the food was delicious, too. You're so lucky!

Helen: We also went to Brazil. It was a really fun country.

John: I haven't been there. Have you been to Argentina?

Helen: No, we haven't. We didn't have time on this trip.

John: It's a nice place. Which other countries have you been to?

Helen: I've been to Japan and China. I want to go to Australia.

John: My brother went to Australia. He loves to travel.

Helen: Which countries has he been to?

John: He has been to South Africa and Kenya.

Helen: I've heard that those are both amazing places.

John: Yes, he wrote a book about traveling there last year.

Helen: They must have been good countries if he wrote a book.

John: That's true. He has also been to Canada and New Zealand.

Helen: Wow! He has really traveled all over the world.

John: Yeah, I think he spends a lot of his time at airports.

Helen: I'm not sure how your brother does it. That seems tiring.

John: I'll ask him next time he wakes up. He's usually sleeping!

Find the mistakes and write the sentence correctly

Helen: Yes, they were bad. We went walking every hour.

_____

Helen: He also went to Canada. It was a really small country.

_____

John: My father went to New Zealand. He hates to travel.

_____

Answer the questions

1. Why is Helen so sleepy?

_____

2. Who did Helen travel with to Mexico?

_____

3. What did Helen do every day on her trip?

_____

4. Where does Helen want to go to?

_____

5. When did John's brother write a book?

_____

Write the answer next to the letter "A"

A: ___ **1.** Helen and her ___ just got back from ___.

a. brother, Australia   b. sister, Japan   c. sister, Mexico   d. aunt, Kenya

A: ___ **2.** The beaches in Mexico were really ___.

a. none   b. great   c. second   d. sleepy

A: ___ **3.** Helen ___ swimming every day.

a. went   b. go   c. been   d. be

A: ___ **4.** Did John like the food in Mexico?

a. Yes, he did.   b. No, he didn't.   c. Yes, he remembers.   d. Yes, he can.

A: ___ **5.** Where else did Helen travel to?

a. Canada.   b. Australia.   c. South Africa.   d. Brazil.

A: ___ **6.** Helen ___ heard that ___ is amazing.

a. have, Canada   b. is, China   c. has, Japan   d. has, Kenya

A: ___ **7.** John's brother ___ a book last ___.

a. read, month   b. wrote, year   c. bought, week   d. written, year

A: ___ **8.** John's brother spends a lot of time at ___.

a. New Zealand   b. airports   c. Canada   d. home

Answers on page 373

Lesson 36: Landscapes

ландшафты

What had you prepared for yesterday's math class?

I had prepared a video about lakes.

Learn the words

1. **river**
   река
2. **beach (es)**
   пляж
3. **mountain**
   гора
4. **volcano (es)**
   вулкан
5. **forest**
   лес

6. **lake**
   озеро
7. **waterfall**
   водопад
8. **island**
   остров
9. **ocean**
   океан
10. **jungle**
    джунгли

Learn a verb

prepare – preparing – prepared – prepared готовить

Mary: Had you prepared anything for yesterday's geography class?

Learn an idiom

A drop in the ocean

Meaning: To only make a tiny impact.

"We donated money to the victims of the tsunami, but I'm afraid it is just *a drop in the ocean*."

Conversation

Tom: Last week in science class, we were talking about pollution.

Mary: Do you mean pollution in the oceans and lakes?

Tom: Yeah, and it's also polluted in the forests.

Mary: Well, we started a group to help clean up the beaches.

Tom: It's a good start, but it's just a drop in the ocean.

Mary: It sounds like you really want to change things.

Tom: I do, but then I forgot to do my other homework.

Mary: Had you prepared anything for yesterday's geography class?

Tom: No, I hadn't. What had you prepared for yesterday's class?

Mary: I had prepared a video about volcanoes and waterfalls.

Tom: Had you prepared anything for yesterday's history class?

Mary: Yes, I had written a speech and article about a mountain.

Tom: What had our classmates prepared for yesterday's class?

Mary: They had made a poster about jungles and islands.

Tom: I think I'm the only one that hadn't prepared anything.

Mary: Yes, but you were thinking about cleaning our landscapes.

Tom: I could have made a presentation on pollution.

Mary: It's an important subject. Some rivers are really dirty.

Tom: The teacher was angry I hadn't done my homework.

Mary: Maybe she'll be happy if you prepare a video about pollution.

Tom: That's true. I can also prepare a quiz to give the class.

Mary: I'm pretty sure the other students don't like quizzes.

Tom: That's a good point, but I think the teacher likes them.

Put the sentences in order

Mary: Had you prepared anything for yesterday's class? ____

Mary: Well, we started a group to help clean up the beaches. ____

Tom: I do, but then I forgot to do my other homework. ____

Mary: Do you mean pollution in the oceans and lakes? ____

Tom: No, I hadn't. What had you prepared for class? ____

Tom: Yeah, and it's also polluted in the forests. ____

Mary: It sounds like you really want to change things. ____

Tom: It's a good start, but it's just a drop in the ocean. ____

Answer the questions

1. In which class were they talking about pollution?

_____

2. What kind of group did Mary start?

_____

3. What had Mary prepared for geography class?

_____

4. Why hadn't Tom prepared anything?

_____

5. Who doesn't like quizzes?

_____

Write the answer next to the letter "A"

A: ___ **1.** Tom talked about pollution last ___ in ___ class.

a. week, geography   b. week, science   c. year, history   d. month, science

A: ___ **2.** Tom feels that cleaning the beaches is just a drop in the ___.

a. lake   b. forest   c. ocean   d. waterfall

A: ___ **3.** Mary had ___ a ___ for history class.

a. prepared, video   b. make, article   c. prepared, speech   d. made, poster

A: ___ **4.** Had Tom prepared anything for geography class?

a. No, he hadn't.   b. Yes, he had.   c. No, I hadn't.   d. No, he doesn't.

A: ___ **5.** ___ was the only one that ___ prepared anything.

a. Classmates, had   b. Teacher, really   c. Students, didn't   d. Tom, hadn't

A: ___ **6.** The teacher was angry he hadn't ___ his homework.

a. preparing   b. done   c. present   d. give

A: ___ **7.** Their classmates had prepared a ___ about ___.

a. video, lakes b. speech, volcanoes c. article, mountains d. poster, islands

A: ___ **8.** Who does Tom think likes quizzes?

a. Other students.   b. Classmates.   c. The teacher.   d. Mary.

Answers on page 373

Lesson 37: Everyday life

повседневная жизнь

When will you have woken up by?

I will have woken up by six o'clock.

Learn the words

1. woken up
проснулся, проснулась

2. brushed my teeth
почистил / почистила зубы

3. done homework
сделал /сделала домашнее задание

4. cooked dinner
приготовил / приготовила ужин

5. taken out the trash
вынес мусор, вынесла мусор

6. eaten breakfast
позавтракал, позавтракала

7. gone to school
пошел / пошла в школу

8. taken a shower
принял душ, принял душ

9. gone to sleep
отправился / отправилась спать

10. gone shopping
пошел / пошла за покупками

Learn a verb

wake – waking – woke – woken будить

Ted: I will have woken up by a quarter past five.

Learn an idiom

Hit the nail on the head

Meaning: To say something that is correct.

"I agree with what you said. You really *hit the nail on the head*."

Kevin: I just saw a TV show about planning everyday life.

Ted: Did it say that people should organize their time well?

Kevin: Yes! You hit the nail on the head!

Ted: It's a really good idea. Let's plan what we'll do this week.

Kevin: Okay. Tomorrow morning, when will you have woken up by?

Ted: I will have woken up by a quarter past five.

Kevin: That's early. Will you have taken a shower by six o'clock?

Ted: Yes, I will have, and I'll have eaten breakfast by half past six.

Kevin: That seems like a really good start to the day.

Ted: That's right, and I will have taken out the trash, too.

Kevin: Are you sure? I've never seen you wake up so early.

Ted: You're right. Actually, I'll probably have gone to school late.

Kevin: Yeah, it's not so easy to be as organized as I am.

Ted: Are you saying that you're better at planning things?

Kevin: Yes. I think I'm much more organized than you are.

Ted: That's not true! I think I always get things done!

Kevin: Really? What time will you have gone to sleep tonight?

Ted: I'll have brushed my teeth and gone to sleep by ten o'clock.

Kevin: Maybe that's true, but will you have done your homework?

Ted: Probably not, but that's because I like video games so much.

Kevin: I think you really need to plan your time better.

Ted: No, I just think the days are too short. I never have time.

Kevin: Here's a secret: the days are longer if you wake up earlier.

Fill in the blanks

Kevin: _____ morning, when will you have _____ up by?

Ted: I will _____ woken up by a _____ past five.

Kevin: Will you have _____ a shower by six _____?

Ted: Yes, and I'll have _____ breakfast by _____ past six.

Kevin: That _____ like a really good _____ to the day.

Ted: _____ right, and I will have taken out the _____, too.

Kevin: Are you _____? I've never _____ you wake up early.

Answer the questions

1. When will Ted have woken up by tomorrow morning?

_____

2. What will Ted have done by six o'clock?

_____

3. Why won't Ted have done his homework?

_____

4. Who has never woken up early?

_____

5. When will Ted have eaten breakfast by?

_____

Write the answer next to the letter "A"

A: ___ **1.** Kevin's TV show was about ___ everyday life.

a. planning   b. hitting nails in   c. eating breakfast in   d. waking up for

A: ___ **2.** Ted will have ___ breakfast by a ___ past six.

a. ate, half   b. eaten, half   c. eat, quarter   d. eating, ten

A: ___ **3.** Will Ted have taken a shower by six o'clock?

a. Yes, he has.   b. No, he hasn't.   c. No, he didn't.   d. Yes, he will have.

A: ___ **4.** Kevin has never ___ Ted ___ up so early.

a. saw, wakes   b. seeing, woke   c. seen, wake   d. see, waking

A: ___ **5.** Kevin ___ he is ___ more organized than Ted is.

a. thinks, much   b. think, much   c. thought, better   d. think, way

A: ___ **6.** Will Ted have gone to sleep by nine o'clock tonight?

a. Yes, he will have. b. Yes, he does. c. No, he can't.   d. No, he won't have.

A: ___ **7.** Ted ___ he never ___ enough time.

a. feels, have   b. feels, has   c. thinks, does   d. says, having

A: ___ **8.** When will Ted have brushed his teeth by?

a. Half past six.   b. A quarter past five.   c. Ten o'clock.   d. Six o'clock.

Answers on page 373

Lesson 38: Languages

языки

How long have you been learning German?

I have been learning German for one year.

Learn the words

1. **English**
   английский
2. **German**
   немецкий
3. **Portuguese**
   португальский
4. **Japanese**
   японский
5. **Vietnamese**
   вьетнамский

6. **Spanish**
   испанский
7. **French**
   французский
8. **Chinese**
   китайский
9. **Hindi**
   хинди
10. **Arabic**
    арабский

Learn a verb

speak – speaking – spoke – spoken говорить

Helen: He has been speaking it for six months. He loves it.

Learn an idiom

Speak the same language

Meaning: To share the same understanding and be in agreement.

"I agree with everything you are saying. I think we're *speaking the same language*."

Jessica: I just came from the library. Your brother was there.

Helen: Yeah, he has a language class. He's learning German.

Jessica: How long has he been studying German?

Helen: He has been speaking it for six months. He loves it.

Jessica: I heard there are many language classes at the library.

Helen: Yes, I know they have Hindi, Portuguese and French, too.

Jessica: My aunt and uncle started learning Japanese.

Helen: Have they been studying Japanese for a long time?

Jessica: No, they haven't been. I think they started last spring.

Helen: They must like languages. They also speak Vietnamese.

Jessica: It's a fun hobby. In school we had to study languages.

Helen: Did you learn Arabic, Chinese, or Spanish?

Jessica: I learned some Arabic and some Spanish, actually.

Helen: How long have you been studying Spanish?

Jessica: I have been learning Spanish for four years.

Helen: That's great! It's very useful to speak other languages.

Jessica: Yes, I like to watch Spanish movies in my free time.

Helen: Speaking of movies, do you want to go to the cinema?

Jessica: Great idea! We can also get some food and drinks.

Helen: Nice! I think we're speaking the same language now.

Jessica: So, which film do you want to watch?

Helen: I know you like Spanish movies, but I don't speak it.

Jessica: No problem! We'll watch an English movie.

Unscramble the sentences

1. been / German / he / studying / long / has / How

_____

2. studying / they / time / been / a / Have / for / Japanese / long

_____

3. have / Spanish / years / for / I / learning / been / four

_____

Answer the questions

1. Where did Jessica see Helen's brother?

_____

2. When did Jessica's aunt and uncle start learning Japanese?

_____

3. How long has Jessica been learning Spanish?

_____

4. Who likes to watch Spanish movies?

_____

5. What did Helen say was very useful?

_____

Write the answer next to the letter "A"

A: ___ **1.** There are many language classes at the ___ .

a. cinema b. spring c. school d. library

A: ___ **2.** Jessica's aunt is learning ___ .

a. Spanish b. German c. Japanese d. French

A: ___ **3.** Helen's brother has been learning German ___ .

a. since spring b. for four years c. for six months d. a long time

A: ___ **4.** Jessica's aunt and uncle ___ been learning for a long time.

a. hasn't b. have c. has d. haven't

A: ___ **5.** Jessica learned some ___ in ___ .

a. Hindi, library b. Arabic, school c. Spanish, cinema d. German, spring

A: ___ **6.** She has been ___ Spanish for four years.

a. learning b. spoken c. learned d. studies

A: ___ **7.** Helen ___ it's ___ to speak other languages.

a. saying, great b. studies, fun c. learned, love d. thinks, useful

A: ___ **8.** Helen ___ speak Spanish.

a. don't b. do c. doesn't d. does

Answers on page 373

Lesson 39: Pets

домашние любимцы

What is faster than a mouse?
A rabbit is faster than a mouse.

Learn the words

1. dog
собака
2. fish
рыба
3. bird
птица
4. rabbit
кролик
5. guinea pig
морская свинка

6. cat
кошка
7. turtle
черепаха
8. mouse
мышь
9. hamster
хомяк
10. snake
змея

Learn a verb

feed – feeding – fed – fed кормить

Jason: Yes, it is. And I have to feed it a lot of food every day.

Learn an idiom

The teacher's pet

Meaning: A student whom the teacher favors.

"Her classmates are jealous of her because she is *the teacher's pet.*"

Emily: Do you know a lot about animals?

Jason: I love animals! I even have a pet hamster.

Emily: Is a hamster more expensive than a mouse?

Jason: Yes, it is. And I have to feed it a lot of food every day.

Emily: Yesterday at school, we were learning about animals.

Jason: You're the teacher's pet! I guess you knew all the answers.

Emily: I just like to study more than other students do.

Jason: Did you talk about dogs and cats?

Emily: Yes, and we also learned about birds and guinea pigs.

Jason: I like all animals, but I like smaller ones better.

Emily: Yes, they're easier and cheaper to have as a pet.

Jason: So as a pet, what is better than a hamster?

Emily: A fish is more colorful than a hamster. I like fish better.

Jason: Is a snake is worse than a turtle?

Emily: Yes, it is. I don't like snakes at all! I saw a scary one on TV.

Jason: A turtle is slower than a snake. I think that's boring.

Emily: I don't like pets that are bigger than a rabbit.

Jason: What is bigger than a rabbit?

Emily: A dog is bigger than a rabbit, and it's faster, too.

Jason: I like dogs. My grandfather walks his dogs at the park.

Emily: People really have personalities just like their pets.

Jason: Do you mean how my grandfather and dogs like exercise?

Emily: Yes, and how you and your hamster like to eat a lot.

Find the mistakes and write the sentence correctly

Emily: Last week at the park we were learning about pets.

_____

Jason: I hate all animals, but she likes bigger ones better.

_____

Jason: Is a fish is cheaper than a bird?

_____

Answer the questions

1. When was Emily learning about animals?

_____

2. What does Emily like better than a hamster?

_____

3. Who thinks turtles are boring?

_____

4. Where does Jason's grandfather go walking?

_____

5. Why doesn't Emily like snakes?

_____

Write the answer next to the letter "A"

A: ___ **1.** Jason ___ to ___ his hamster every day.

a. have, fed   b. is, feeding   c. does, feed   d. has, feed

A: ___ **2.** Where was Emily talking about dogs and cats?

a. The park.   b. At school.   c. On TV.   d. At the pet store.

A: ___ **3.** Who has dogs as pets?

a. Emily.   b. The teacher.   c. Jason's grandfather.   d. Jason.

A: ___ **4.** Is a fish more colorful than a hamster?

a. Yes, it is.   b. No, it's not.   c. Yes, it does.   d. No, it can't.

A: ___ **5.** Emily ___ a snake is ___ than a turtle.

a. saw, scary   b. thinks, worse   c. thinks, better   d. likes, smaller

A: ___ **6.** Jason thinks a turtle is ___ because it's ___ than a snake.

a. better, smaller   b. great, bigger   c. boring, slower   d. scary, faster

A: ___ **7.** Emily ___ like ___ pets.

a. don't, dog   b. doesn't, expensive   c. can't, faster   d. doesn't, bigger

A: ___ **8.** Jason thinks a ___ is more expensive than a ___.

a. mouse, hamster   b. turtle, snake   c. rabbit, dog   d. hamster, mouse

Answers on page 373

Lesson 40: Fast food

фаст-фуд

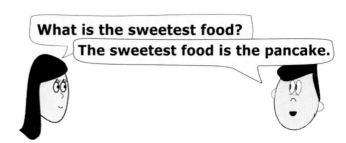

What is the sweetest food?
The sweetest food is the pancake.

Learn the words

1. **doughnut**
   бублик
2. **cheeseburger**
   чизбургер
3. **chicken nuggets**
   куриные наггеты
4. **pancake**
   блинчик
5. **taco**
   тако

6. **french fries**
   картофель-фри
7. **onion rings**
   колечки лука
8. **hot dog**
   хот-дог
9. **fried chicken**
   жареная курица
10. **burrito**
    буррито

Learn a verb

try – trying – tried – tried пробовать

Ted: Did he say to try the cheeseburger or the hot dog?

Learn an idiom

You are what you eat

Meaning: The food that you eat affects your health.

"Careful not to eat too much fast food. *You are what you eat.*"

Ted: I'm glad we're finally going to eat. I'm really hungry.

Matthew: Kevin told me this fast food restaurant is pretty good.

Ted: Did he say to try the cheeseburger or the hot dog?

Matthew: He said the burrito is the best thing on the menu.

Ted: The burrito is the most expensive! What's the cheapest food?

Matthew: The cheapest food is the taco, but it's also the saltiest.

Ted: Are the onion rings the worst thing? They look unhealthy.

Matthew: Yes, they are. Remember that you are what you eat.

Ted: That's true. I was feeling really tired in gym class last week.

Matthew: We're having fast food today, so it won't be too healthy.

Ted: Okay, so what is the most delicious food?

Matthew: I think the most delicious food is the fried chicken.

Ted: That's harder to eat. I think I'll try the chicken nuggets.

Matthew: Also, let's share some french fries.

Ted: Good idea. Are the pancakes the sweetest?

Matthew: No, they aren't. The doughnuts are the sweetest.

Ted: When I eat fast food, I like to get dessert, too.

Matthew: I want the burrito. Susan ate it on Tuesday and loved it.

Ted: I'll try the hot dog because it looks bigger. I also want a taco.

Matthew: That's a lot of food to eat at once. You're really hungry!

Ted: Well, I didn't eat breakfast this morning because I was late.

Matthew: That's why you should plan your time better.

Ted: I also forgot to bring money, so can I borrow some?

Learn the English

Put the sentences in order

Ted: That's true. I was feeling really tired in gym class. ____

Ted: Are the onion rings the worst thing? They look unhealthy. ____

Matthew: He said the burrito is the best thing on the menu. ____

Matthew: Yes, they are. Remember that you are what you eat. ____

Matthew: The cheapest food is the taco. It's also the saltiest. ____

Ted: The burrito is the most expensive! What's the cheapest? ____

Ted: Did he say to try the cheeseburger or the hot dog? ____

Matthew: We're having fast food so it won't be too healthy. ____

Answer the questions

1. Who wants to eat a burrito?

_____

2. What is the cheapest food?

_____

3. Why is Ted so hungry?

_____

4. When did Susan eat fast food?

_____

5. Which food is the sweetest?

_____

Write the answer next to the letter "A"

A: ___ **1.** Kevin said to ___ the ___.

a. eat, cheeseburger   b. taste, taco   c. try, burrito   d. try, hot dog

A: ___ **2.** Is the taco the saltiest food?

a. Yes, it is.   b. Yes, it has.   c. Yes, it can.   d. No, it's not.

A: ___ **3.** The burrito is the ___ fast food on the menu.

a. cheapest   b. most expensive   c. saltiest   d. sweetest

A: ___ **4.** Ted was feeling ___ last ___.

a. happy, Tuesday   b. late, night   c. hungry, Tuesday   d. tired, week

A: ___ **5.** They are having fast food ___.

a. last week   b. today   c. on Tuesday   d. for breakfast

A: ___ **6.** The most ___ food is the fried chicken.

a. expensive   b. best   c. cheapest   d. delicious

A: ___ **7.** Who loved the burrito?

a. Kevin.   b. Matthew.   c. Susan.   d. Ted.

A: ___ **8.** Matthew and Ted are going to share the ___.

a. french fries   b. fried chicken   c. onion rings   d. chicken nuggets

Answers on page 373

Answers

Lesson 1 test	1. c 2. a 3. b 4. b 5. d 6. b 7. c 8. b
Lesson 2 test	1. b 2. b 3. d 4. b 5. d 6. c 7. a 8. d
Lesson 3 test	1. b 2. c 3. a 4. d 5. d 6. b 7. a 8. d
Lesson 4 test	1. b 2. a 3. b 4. d 5. c 6. c 7. d 8. d
Lesson 5 test	1. b 2. d 3. c 4. b 5. b 6. a 7. d 8. a
Lesson 6 test	1. b 2. a 3. a 4. c 5. d 6. c 7. b 8. a
Lesson 7 test	1. b 2. d 3. a 4. a 5. c 6. c 7. d 8. a
Lesson 8 test	1. b 2. d 3. b 4. c 5. c 6. a 7. c 8. b
Lesson 9 test	1. d 2. a 3. b 4. d 5. c 6. d 7. a 8. c
Lesson 10 test	1. b 2. a 3. c 4. a 5. b 6. c 7. a 8. d
Lesson 11 test	1. b 2. c 3. b 4. a 5. d 6. d 7. a 8. c
Lesson 12 test	1. d 2. a 3. b 4. c 5. c 6. b 7. a 8. d
Lesson 13 test	1. d 2. d 3. b 4. b 5. c 6. d 7. a 8. c
Lesson 14 test	1. b 2. b 3. c 4. d 5. a 6. a 7. c 8. d
Lesson 15 test	1. d 2. b 3. d 4. a 5. c 6. c 7. a 8. b
Lesson 16 test	1. b 2. d 3. a 4. a 5. b 6. c 7. d 8. c
Lesson 17 test	1. a 2. d 3. a 4. c 5. c 6. b 7. b 8. c
Lesson 18 test	1. a 2. c 3. d 4. c 5. d 6. b 7. b 8. a
Lesson 19 test	1. c 2. a 3. c 4. b 5. d 6. d 7. a 8. d
Lesson 20 test	1. c 2. a 3. c 4. d 5. b 6. b 7. d 8. a

Lesson 21 test	1. a	2. c	3. d	4. d	5. b	6. d	7. c	8. b
Lesson 22 test	1. c	2. d	3. b	4. c	5. c	6. a	7. b	8. a
Lesson 23 test	1. b	2. c	3. b	4. d	5. a	6. d	7. a	8. b
Lesson 24 test	1. d	2. b	3. b	4. a	5. c	6. d	7. c	8. a
Lesson 25 test	1. d	2. b	3. a	4. b	5. d	6. c	7. c	8. a
Lesson 26 test	1. d	2. c	3. b	4. b	5. b	6. c	7. a	8. b
Lesson 27 test	1. b	2. d	3. d	4. b	5. a	6. c	7. c	8. a
Lesson 28 test	1. c	2. b	3. c	4. d	5. d	6. c	7. a	8. b
Lesson 29 test	1. d	2. b	3. b	4. a	5. c	6. b	7. a	8. b
Lesson 30 test	1. d	2. b	3. c	4. a	5. d	6. b	7. b	8. c
Lesson 31 test	1. a	2. d	3. d	4. b	5. c	6. c	7. b	8. c
Lesson 32 test	1. d	2. a	3. b	4. c	5. c	6. b	7. a	8. d
Lesson 33 test	1. c	2. d	3. c	4. b	5. b	6. a	7. d	8. a
Lesson 34 test	1. b	2. d	3. b	4. d	5. c	6. c	7. a	8. a
Lesson 35 test	1. c	2. b	3. a	4. a	5. d	6. d	7. b	8. b
Lesson 36 test	1. b	2. c	3. c	4. a	5. d	6. b	7. d	8. c
Lesson 37 test	1. a	2. b	3. d	4. c	5. a	6. d	7. b	8. c
Lesson 38 test	1. d	2. c	3. c	4. d	5. b	6. a	7. d	8. c
Lesson 39 test	1. d	2. b	3. c	4. a	5. b	6. c	7. d	8. d
Lesson 40 test	1. c	2. a	3. b	4. d	5. b	6. d	7. c	8. a

Made in United States
North Haven, CT
27 October 2021

10627173R00205